Just Call Me "Teacher"

A Memoir about My Career as a Correctional Educator

Rosemary Pineau

 FriesenPress

Suite 300 - 990 Fort St
Victoria, BC, V8V 3K2
Canada

www.friesenpress.com

ISBN
978-1-5255-9515-8 (Hardcover)
978-1-5255-9514-1 (Paperback)
978-1-5255-9516-5 (eBook)

1. BISAC *Biography & Autobiography, Educators*

Distributed to the trade by The Ingram Book Company

To my husband, Barry—hang on, the ride's not over yet …

Table of Contents

PREFACE

In Canada, all of the federal correctional institutions (prisons) have an on-site school. The Correctional Service of Canada calls their instructors "correctional educators." But I like to be known as a *teacher*. I believe that this word is the best descriptor.

The purpose of this book is to highlight some of my experiences as a teacher in a minimum-security federal prison for men. Prisons do not get a lot of attention from the public unless there is some sensational incident, which is usually negative. I would like people to know that there are some very positive things happening in our Canadian prisons. Of course, there are some people who cannot be rehabilitated, and that is unfortunate. But for those who may have the possibility of turning their lives around, I am thankful that I got to be a small part of that during my 25 years working at Westmorland Institution in Dorchester, New Brunswick.

I have used random first names for all of the inmates included in my book in an effort to protect the privacy of these individuals. I am not naive enough to believe that everyone I taught or came into contact with during this time went on to lead successful lives. I am hopeful that—due to further education—a lot of them became productive citizens in their respective communities.

I used full names for staff members, colleagues, and superiors, except where I could not remember full names. Where I did not use a name, I referred to the person by his or her work title.

For my part, I very much enjoyed working at Westmorland Institution with my colleagues and with the inmates. This will become apparent as you read my excerpts. Thank you for keeping an open mind. I am sure you will find some of my experiences entertaining.

INTRODUCTION
A Little about Me

My name is Rosemary Alice Pineau (née McAtee). I was born to Robert and Kathleen (Rush) McAtee, on June 3, 1951, in Millinocket, Maine. I grew up in a paper mill town; its claim to fame has always been that it lies at the base of Mount Katahdin, just at the northern end of the 2,000-mile Appalachian Trail. There was a boom in the paper industry while I was growing up and because of that, Millinocket was a thriving little town.

I attended St. Martin of Tours Parochial School from kindergarten through Grade 9. Then I attended my mother's alma mater, George W. Stearns High School. I even had a teacher, Miss Griffin, who also had taught my mother.

I am the eldest of six children, and I grew up with four brothers: Bob, Bill, Rick, and Mike. My baby sister, Madolyn, was born when I was 17, but I only lived at home for the first year of her life. I often returned home to visit, but I never lived there again.

I attended the University of Prince Edward Island (UPEI) in Charlottetown, Prince Edward Island, Canada. After four years, I graduated from the Bachelor of Education Program with a major in French and a minor in Spanish. I really wanted to be a teacher. I had loved school right from kindergarten. What could be better in life than to be surrounded by books, learning, teaching, reading, and so forth?

I got my first teaching job on the Island at Cornwall Junior High School, located in a small town of the same name. This was perfect because I had just married my soulmate, Barry Pineau, whom I had met at UPEI. He still had two more years of undergraduate work to complete at the university.

While Barry spent those two years studying, I taught French at Cornwall Junior High School. The school had 250 students in grades 7 to 9. I was the only French teacher, so I taught all of them.

My first year of teaching was very difficult. I really didn't understand kids, and I really didn't get that a lot of them just didn't want to learn French. After looking all summer for another job, I returned to teach a second year, which was much better because I tried to make learning a little more fun for the students. I made up games using French vocabulary words. I got the students to make one-line sentences in French to describe themselves or something they liked, and had competitions to figure out who had written the sentences. I started a French club, which ran once a week at lunchtime, and planned activities that interested the students. Fun is key and it worked! Thus, teaching became easier for me. I am really glad that I had to return for the second year because I thought that I hated teaching, but I was just inexperienced and hadn't found my style or my way yet.

My second year taught me that I was responsible for igniting the desire to learn in students, even the difficult ones. That became my challenge to myself and since has carried me through all my teaching experiences. Today, I am happy and confident to say that I am an excellent teacher. I believe that I am able to motivate and teach the most unwilling student of any age.

At the end of my second year of teaching at Cornwall, Barry and I packed up and left Canada for a year, so that he could work on his master's degree in guidance counseling at the University of Maine in Orono. I was thrilled to return to my home state, even if only for a year.

We arrived in Orono during the summer of 1975 after Barry received his degree at the University of Prince Edward Island. I looked for a teaching job in Orono and in the surrounding areas. The schools only offered French and Spanish at the high-school level, so jobs were limited. I did a bit of substitute teaching but could not find anything full time.

Since I was unable to find a full-time job, Barry and I decided to start our family. I got pregnant in October 1975 with our first son, Joey. It was a perfect time to be in the United States because 1976 was the bicentennial year, and everybody was in a celebratory mood. There were Minutemen and women in period clothing everywhere. For Christmas in 1975, I made my mom and sister matching long, red dresses, and frilly hats. They looked like they were teleported from 1776.

After Joey was born, on June 27, 1976, we returned to Canada in late August once Barry completed his degree. We rented a house on Wedgewood Avenue in Riverview, New Brunswick. Years later, we bought a house one street down and diagonally across from there. It is where we live to this day.

Barry had secured a job as a guidance counsellor in the greater Moncton area, servicing several elementary schools. At that time, elementary schools offered part-time work for half a day per week at the smaller schools and a full day per week at the larger schools. Today, every school has a full-time guidance counselor at every level.

During this time, I stumbled into tutoring. I started teaching one little boy who was in Grade 2 French immersion. He was having some difficulty reading and spelling. But he was a bright child who only needed a bit of one-to-one attention, which his unilingual parents were unable to give him. He was a pleasure to work with, and he made great progress.

From him, I got the idea that I should teach parents not how to speak French, but how to pronounce French words. Then the parents could dictate spelling and listen to their children's reading to see if they were pronouncing the words correctly. This was sufficient for parents with children in grades 1 to 3 when helping with homework.

As a result, I put together a program, which I called French Pronunciation for Parents of Early Immersion Students, and presented it to the night school director at Riverview High School. I got hired and taught this program—my program—two nights a week for 10 weeks. It was a great success, and I ended up teaching it twice annually for several years. My classes were at full capacity, and I got to meet and help a lot of parents. It was so much fun!

Meanwhile, by word of mouth, I started acquiring more students to tutor. As the years went by, my schedule consisted of two evenings teaching private students, along with two evenings teaching adult night classes. When my program seemed to slow down a bit, I started teaching conversational French to adults twice a week at Riverview High School, and then eventually at Moncton Community College (New Brunswick Community College at the Moncton campus). I taught levels one through four, as needed, at various times.

I really enjoyed both types of teaching—working one-to-one with private students and teaching groups of adults. Most of my private students required help with French reading, spelling, and comprehension. I also worked with some students on English courses. I did not take on math students. Math was not my specialty.

I had been working with a student for a couple of years on French subjects. He had made progress, and I was ready to tell his mom that he probably did not need me anymore. She surprised me by saying he now needed help with math. He went to school at Riverview High School. (I did not tutor math above elementary level.)

I pulled a page from my notebook and started to write. She asked me what I was doing and I told her I would give her the names of a couple of math tutors.

"Oh, no, it has to be you. He only wants to work with you," she said.

I told her that I would get the materials and see if I could be up to the task. The next week was March break, and I would be at my parents' place in Maine. This was in the late 1980s. My sister was still in high school, but she was amazing at math. I decided to enlist her help.

When we started out, she asked:

"Do you know what a radical is?"

"Sure, it's someone who doesn't conform!" I stated proudly.

"No, I'm talking about a math radical," she said.

"Well, then, no, I guess I don't know what a radical is."

"Okay," she said, "that's where we will start."

Madolyn was an amazing teacher, and I learned so much from her. Two important things that she taught me that stood out and that I always used afterwards were: finding out where the student is and teach from there, and not skipping any steps in the procedures being taught (i.e., follow a progression from step one to the end).

Those two pieces of advice guided my own teaching from then on. It was thanks to Madolyn that I was able to work successfully with the student who needed help with math. It was also thanks to her that I qualified for my next venture.

In the meantime, I continued growing my family with two daughters, Aimée and Alicia, and two more sons, Jonathan and Jeffrey. My five children are five bright lights in my life—they are all successful adults now and married with families of their own.

This gives you a glimpse into who I am. My story from here on will concentrate more on my professional life than on my personal one.

CHAPTER 1

How I Became a Correctional Educator

One fall afternoon in 1990, I was waiting with my two little boys, Jon and Jeff, for my three other children, Joey, Aimée, and Alicia, to get home from school, when the phone rang. It was Pauline Vromans, the sister of one of my best friends, Denise Kinnie. Pauline taught at Dorchester Medium-Security Penitentiary in Dorchester, New Brunswick, about 40 minutes from where I live. She told me that they needed an interim teacher at the minimum-security school at Westmorland Institution, which was right next door, on the same hill. She had given my name to Dell Amon, the assistant warden of correctional programs (AWCP). Pauline was calling to tell me that he wanted to interview me, if I would be interested. It would be a two-week job with the school day running from 8 a.m. until 4 p.m. Pauline gave me Dell's phone number and highly encouraged me to call him. I took the number down and told her I would let her know my decision.

When I hung up the phone, I sat down to think this through. As I noted before, I believed that I could teach anything I knew to anybody, and I was confident that I could instill a desire to learn in any candidate as well. I knew that my biggest strength was in remedial work. But I did not know anybody who had been to prison. It is shameful to say it now, but my attitude was that if people committed crimes, they should be locked up and the key should be thrown away. And who would care? Feeling this way, I hesitated in phoning the AWCP.

Finally, I thought that it might be a good learning experience for me to take on the job. After all, it was only for two weeks. Hey, it was all about me, right? I'm kidding, but at that point, it really was. I phoned Dell, talked to him for a few minutes, and found that he was really eager to meet me. He asked if I could meet him at the institution the next day, and I agreed. That evening, I told my husband about the job opportunity. He supported my decision to give it a try.

I met Dell the next day, walked through the school with him, met some of the students, and agreed to return on Monday to teach for the next two weeks. I was impressed by the school, and I was excited to get started and give teaching there a try. But this was totally out of my comfort zone. If Pauline had not thought of recommending me to the AWCP, I never would have thought of applying for the job.

At this point, I had a full schedule of tutoring and teaching in the evenings. I phoned all the parents of my private students, and they were okay with me taking two weeks off—but I assured them that if any child had a major test and needed help, I would go to their aid after receiving a phone call from the parent. As for my adult classes, I was unable to reschedule them, so on those days I worked all day at the prison and taught in the evenings, arriving home at 10:30 p.m. after my own children were already in bed.

Once Monday—my first day teaching at Westmorland Institution—arrived, I got set up in the General Educational Development (GED) classroom. The room was small, with 12 student desks and one large teacher's desk all crammed together. Behind the whiteboard was a good-sized walk-in storage closet that locked. The closet stored books, private papers, tests, and other items, including a phone. This was a classroom, but it was a classroom inside a prison. Some things needed to be locked up to ensure their integrity, such as tests that could become compromised if left lying about. Phones that were able to make outside calls were guarded with the utmost security.

At 8 a.m., my students started arriving. I met 12 men who were working towards their GED. They were all ordinary-looking people, of course, who would not have stood out in the general population of Moncton or any other town or city in North America.

But like any students with a substitute teacher, they tested the limits, and in this setting, they had to determine if I was afraid of them. On the second day, one student arrived late, and I pointed out to him that tardiness was unacceptable.

He marched over to me and yelled in my face, "F—k you!"

Without thinking, I retorted, "In your dreams! Now go sit down and get to work."

He was shocked and reacted by doing exactly what he was told. The rest of the class was graveyard silent for about a minute, and then burst into laughter. I had passed the test. They knew I was not afraid. As I would find out later, my lack of fear not only greatly impressed them, but also allowed me to work well with them and gain their trust. This is the most important first hurdle to clear when working with inmates.

At this point, I had no experience working with inmates, but I had a great deal of experience working with struggling learners.

On the fourth morning with this class, one of the students, Mack, was attentively looking at me. I started to wonder if I had dirt on my face.

"Miss, could I ask you a personal question?" he said.

"You may ask, but I may choose not to answer it," I replied.

"Okay, are those your teeth?"

"What? My teeth? Of course; they're in my mouth."

"But, are they your real teeth, your own teeth?" he persisted.

"Yes, they are my own real teeth."

There was a long pause.

"Wow, Miss, you have very beautiful teeth for a woman your age!" Mack exclaimed.

I was shocked. I was 40 years old. I did not ask how old he thought I was, because I figured I did not want to know.

"Thanks" was all I managed to say.

At that time, there was a bus service from the town of Riverview to the institution. It went from Riverview, picking up staff all along the way through Moncton, Dieppe, Memramcook, College Bridge, and on to Dorchester. Of course, the route reversed for returning home at 4 p.m. It was very economical and saved wear and tear on our own cars. It was also fun to just sit back, drink coffee, and chat on the way to and from work each day.

When I got on the bus that evening, I told the story of the "teeth question" from class that morning. The manager of Supply and Services (SIS), Francis Léger, was sitting next to me. He thought the story was hilarious. For years after that, whenever I saw him, he would ask, "Are those your teeth?" If I saw him from a distance, he would point to his teeth and smile.

My two-week contract with the class turned into five weeks. Six students were to write their GED tests at the end of the fifth week, and Dell implored me to see them through the tests. To me, these men were students first and inmates second. We had formed a mutual respect, we all were working towards the same goals, and we needed each other to be successful.

I even drove the six students, in an institutional van, to Moncton on a Friday evening and all-day Saturday to write the GED tests. I found out later that five of the six students had earned their GED certificates, while the sixth student had achieved four of the five tests with only math to rewrite. I was really pleased, and I was told that all of the students were greatly encouraged by their success.

At the end of the fifth week, I asked Dell about the possibility of staying on as their full-time GED teacher. He told me that the school did not offer full-time teaching contracts, but I could choose to stay on indefinitely with the risk of being let go at any moment without notice—not for doing a bad job—due to the instability of the schools in the Atlantic prison system at the time. Although these 12 students had won my heart, and I enjoyed teaching there very much, I had to walk away. I had a full schedule of teaching students and adult classes in the evenings. These jobs were a sure thing with stability and monetary rewards. I could not let that go to take on an *iffy* job.

So, I said goodbye and walked away from the situation.

Over the next year, 1990, at Westmorland Institution, there was great instability, a lack of resources, stress, and lots of ups and downs for its teachers. It was a transitional period where Correctional Service of Canada (CSC) was trying to decide if it would hire teachers as CSC employees or continue to contract educational services through private companies. Throughout this time at Westmorland Institution, teachers were on individual personal service contracts and were only paid on a monthly basis. I do not know all the details of their contracts. These contracts were for one year, and the teachers did not know what would happen at the end of that duration. It was uncertain if they would be able to retain their jobs or if they would need to compete for them.

I got the chance to substitute teach there several times in both the level two (grades 7 and 8 math, English and science) and GED classes. Although literacy is not one of my main teaching interests, I would have substituted in the literacy class as well. However, for whatever reason, I was never asked to fill in. Substituting at Westmorland Institution was not stressful for me, but I could see how unsettled the full-time teachers were, and I was inwardly happy with the decision I had made not to work there full-time during this upheaval.

This is an explanation of terms. The education provider owns a company for which he competes for a contract to provide education within the prison. He employs and pays teachers to provide those educational services. He is responsible for making sure that the teachers are following rules and doing a good job and, of course, he pays the salaries. He is not usually on site, but periodically checks in to make sure there are no problems. On a day-to-day basis, teachers answer to the head teacher, if the education provider employs one. (Some companies rely on a head teacher who carries out extra duties as required by the company. Other companies do not provide head teachers, in which case the owner of the company would have full responsibility although absent from the site.) For on-site issues, teachers may refer to the AWCP.

CSC is known for its acronyms, which I will explain as I use them. Every department has a three-or four-letter acronym and sometimes even employees are lost to explain what the acronym means, although all workers know what services are provided by each one. Sometimes, when at home talking to my husband, I would use an acronym and he would ask what I was talking about, completely throwing me off my story.

Nearing the end of that school year in 1991, CSC decided to contract a company to provide educational services. I heard that the education provider for Dorchester Medium-Security Penitentiary, Bill Snowdon, owner of Marshland Educational Services, was also taking over the education services at Westmorland Minimum-Security Institution. I knew this gentleman, and had met him quite a few times. I phoned him and asked him to consider hiring me for one of the teaching positions. He told me that he would only need one teacher: a teacher for level two. But he had already promised the job to someone else. Although I was disappointed, I told him to call on me any time to substitute in any class at medium- or minimum-security prison.

Over the next couple of weeks into summer 1991, I vacationed with my five children at my mother's camp in Maine. When I returned home in mid-July, I got a call from Bill asking me if I wanted to work for him starting August 1. I asked how long a stint it would be, and he told me he would hire me full time, if I wanted the job. It had not worked out with the person to whom he had originally promised the job, and I was next in line. Bill told me that I would be working at the minimum-security institution (Westmorland) for three months, and then he would need me at the medium-security prison (Dorchester) after that. I was over the moon with excitement. Just when it suited me and my family, I had a full-time job doing what I loved—teaching—and more specifically, remedial teaching. What could be better than that?

So, on August 1, I showed up at Westmorland Minimum-Security Institution and started working with *my class*: level two. I loved everything about it right from the start. Let me explain about Canada's correctional system at that time. It was all about rehabilitation. The fact is that in Canada, most inmates eventually get released. Now, would you want one of these men living next door to you feeling like a contributing, rehabilitated member of society, or feeling like a hurt, resentful, angry, and vengeful outcast? I would definitely prefer the former, and that was CSC's mandate.

All of the prison staff made up the team that was tasked with molding these inmates into the best law-abiding people possible. At the school, we also took this seriously and were well-equipped to do our part of the job. We treated the inmates as students first and inmates second. Don't get me wrong, though. We were all trained in dynamic security and guarded against rule-breaking and contraband. We were taught how to detect when we were being played or conned, and we worked towards rehabilitation in those areas as well. But because of the great backup from the correctional officers and other security people, we were free to teach.

Right from the start, I loved teaching the level two class. In public school teaching, this was also my favorite level to teach. I really liked the subject matter at this level, and I enjoyed the beginnings of independence shown by the students. I was always impressed when students began taking responsibility for their own learning and started using the teacher as a guide, rather than a parent figure.

I reminded myself not to get too attached to this group of students. I knew I would be leaving this class and this institution before too long.

But as it turned out, Bill recognized that I worked well with my two colleagues: the GED teacher, Pam Oulton, and the literacy teacher, Kim Hendrickson. He thought it would be best to keep what he called "a well-oiled team" together.

I was thrilled with his decision and settled in for what I hoped would be a long career teaching the level two class at Westmorland Institution. Hindsight is 20/20. At the time, I didn't realize that I would work there for 25 years, despite changes within CSC, contraction of services, and changes both good and bad, but mostly good.

As a classroom teacher, I always had very few rules, believing that the more formal rules were implemented, the more it would be a challenge for the students to break the rules and see how much they could get away with. I made a sign and hung it up just to the left of the door inside of my classroom. It read:

The Three Rs
- Respect for self
- Respect for others
- Responsibility for own actions

Whenever I welcomed new students, I would tell them that following this sign was a must in my classroom. Later in this book, I will tell you how this led to a funny incident.

CHAPTER 2

Canadian Federal Prison

In Canada, offenders who are sentenced to up to two years less a day serve their time in provincial jails. Those who are sentenced to two years or more serve their time in federal prison.

There are three basic levels of federal prison, which are based on the risk and needs of the individual. The levels include minimum, medium, and maximum security. All who are sentenced federally begin their sentences at a regional reception institution. Here in Atlantic Canada, that institution is Springhill Institution, located in Springhill, Nova Scotia. At Springhill they are assessed for security risk and their needs based on criminogenic factors. (Before being placed in the appropriate prison, the individuals are referred to as *offenders*. Afterwards, they are referred to as *inmates*. Once they are released on parole, they are referred to as *offenders* or *parolees* until the expiry of their full sentence.)

The offender's *static* risk level is based on:
- their criminal history
- details of use of violence and sex offending
- the results of the recidivism prediction scale (SIR-R1).

The offender's *dynamic* risk factor is based on seven dynamic risk areas:
- employment
- marital/family
- associates/social interaction
- substance abuse

- community functioning
- personal/emotional orientation
- attitude

For each of these areas, case managers flag indicators and rate the severity of need. When all the assessments are made, the case manager makes a correctional case plan to address the needs and correct the deficits where possible.

The Commissioner's Directive 720 (CD 720) deals with programs and education. Looking at the education part of this directive, it states that if an inmate does not have a high-school diploma or a GED certificate, school should be on his case plan. The directive outlines the responsibilities of all concerned, starting with the assistant commissioner, Correctional Operations and Programs; the director general, Offender Programs and Reintegration; the regional deputy commissioner; the regional administrator; the institutional head; the manager with the Chief of Education; the teacher; the parole officer; the librarian; and the inmate.

All the above people are involved in the planning and implementation of each inmate's correctional case plan. I will not expand on any of the above, but I wanted to indicate how much planning and work goes into assuring that each and every individual has a case plan put into action. If school is on his case plan, he must attend school unless there is a good reason for him not to do so, as determined by his case-management team.

Sometimes in the past, offenders had trouble in school and were left behind. In those cases, many of them dropped out of school and never wanted to take it up again, viewing it as a time of failure that they were not willingly going to repeat. Often, students are led to believe that they are incapable of learning, even if it is not the intention of the teacher or administrator to make them feel that way. Students often compare themselves to other students and feel inadequate witnessing others learning easily, when it is just so difficult for them.

Sometimes it is just a matter of coming in contact with someone who is able to assess and remediate a learning difficulty. Grant you, sometimes they are diagnosed with a learning disability. In my experience, there are a lot of people who have learning *difficulties* and very few who have true learning *disabilities* (meaning they are incapable of learning, even when taught). I have concentrated here on the education aspect but, as noted, there are many other factors that are taken into account when making a correctional case plan.

Once all aspects of the many assessments are taken into account, the offender gets placed at the federal institution that is the least restrictive possible. There, he will work at rehabilitation with the end result being reintegration into the community.

A couple of documents that are very important for CSC are the Corrections and Conditional Release Act (CCRA), which was first brought into law on June 18, 1992, and its mission statement, which was first implemented in 1989. Over the years, both documents have been amended and updated. These are two documents that guide CSC.

The CCRA contains principles that guide how CSC achieves its mandate. These include:

- the protection of society
- the nature and gravity of an offense and the offender's degree of responsibility
- rights and privileges for offenders
- the concept of measures that are "limited only to what is necessary and proportionate to attain the purposes of this Act."

As you may have noticed, this Act is to protect society, first and foremost, and then to look out for the offender's needs and rights. The Act very specifically lays out how CSC should get from step one to the end. I am not going to expand on all of these steps, but I wanted to clarify that housing inmates is not done lightly or on a whim. Very specific guidelines are in place and are adhered to by all staff.

This is CSC's Mission Statement:
"The Correctional Service of Canada, as part of the criminal justice system and respecting the rule of law, contributes to the protection of society by actively encouraging and assisting offenders to become law-abiding citizens, while exercising reasonable, safe, secure and humane control."

The mission statement contains five core values. Here, they are paraphrased:

1. Respect the dignity of individuals.

2. Recognize that the offender has the potential to live as a law-abiding citizen.

3. Recognize that our staff is our strength and major resource.

4. Share ideas, knowledge, values and experience, nationally and internationally.

5. Manage the Service with openness and integrity and be accountable to the solicitor general.

When new employees start working at a federal facility, they are scheduled to take mission statement training. Everyone needs to be aware of CSC's core values and the strategic objectives.

This has been a quick overview of the rules and guidelines for CSC. You will notice that on a day-to-day basis, I do not mention these guidelines, although in everything we do as correctional educators, those guidelines are in the back of our minds. As mentioned, we are all supposed to be on the same page in working towards rehabilitation to ensure successful reintegration.

CHAPTER 3

Minimum Security

In Canada, most minimum-security prisons are releasing institutions, meaning that it is the last stop for inmates before being released back into the community. For this reason, inmates are encouraged to follow their correctional plan to do their best to prepare for the outside world. At Westmorland Institution, inmates live in condo-like buildings with six to eight occupants. Within their unit, they are expected to perform all the necessary tasks that one would to live a good, productive life. They are responsible for ordering their food for the week, collecting it, storing it, and cooking it. They are expected to keep the house clean, as all occupants share chores within the common areas and keep their own rooms tidy.

Although, minimum-security facilities are federal prisons, there are no fences. Inmates know the boundaries and what is *off limits*. They are honor-bound to stay within the limits and the reward for doing so is that they are able to live in housing units rather than cells. If they decide to leave the premises, they do not escape, they merely walk away. But if they are found to be at large, their security rating will be re-evaluated and they will not be eligible to return to minimum-security.

Inmates are free to come and go around the compound from the 7:30 a.m. head count until the 10 p.m. head count. During the day, they are expected to work an eight-hour shift. They are assigned to a program or a worksite—school is considered both a worksite and a program. Inmates may spend the whole day at one site or split time between two sites. Sometimes, they will spend a half day in a program or school and the other half working.

After 10 p.m., they are expected to stay in their units until 7:30 a.m. If they attempt to leave, the alarmed door will sound an alert in the Control Center. Inmates are subject to head counts five times a day, including two *stand-to counts*, where they must stand at their bedroom door. For the overnight count, they do not have to leave their beds. Instead, the officer will shine a light into their bedroom window and proceed from there. Each condo is equipped with a phone that calls the Control Center in the case of an emergency.

At minimum-security prisons, activities are usually planned for the inmates during off-work hours. There is a fully equipped gym, a games room, a ceramic shop, a crafts and woodworking room, a well-stocked library, etc. Inmates are encouraged to be active during their downtime by exercising, socializing, and reading. There is a social programs officer on duty throughout the evening until the 10 p.m. count. Frank Landry has held this position at Westmorland Institution for 40 years. He is also in charge of processing clearances for volunteers to come in and interact with the inmates and escort them on temporary absences. Sometimes he facilitates events with guests from the community for various social gatherings or sports competitions with inmates competing against the public.

In all federal prisons in Canada, there is a vast array of inmates serving time for every type of crime. Minimum security does not relate only to white-collar crime. While I was working at Westmorland Institution, there were between 225 and 275 inmates. Approximately 70 of those were "lifers," people who had taken at least one life and had spent seven to 30 years in medium security. Through a strict progression and following their case plans, they had *cascaded* down from higher security and could now be managed in a minimum-security setting. About two-thirds of the population were violent offenders or sex offenders. There were between 15 and 20 gang members, 75 more or less first-timers and punks, some inmates who had committed robberies, fraud, and property offenses, and finally 15 to 20 "old guys."

Some of the inmates may be "institutionalized" and this brings challenges for the teacher or manager, considering these inmates may have severe impairment in the areas of perception, emotions, survival tactics, etc.

Lifers are sometimes granted parole after serving their minimum as given by the judge; i.e., life 10, life 20, or life 25. Once a lifer has done his minimum amount of time, he is eligible to apply for parole. There is a process for this. He must complete packages of temporary absences, first escorted, then unescorted; and he must complete a series of temporary absences where he stays in a halfway house for a night or two. Then he may apply to go before the Parole Board of Canada; if the board members believe that he may be managed in the community, they will grant him day parole. This process is long and complicated, and the parole officer makes sure that the inmate has successfully completed all of the steps in the process before being presented to the Parole Board of Canada. A lifer must be accountable for the rest of his life and may be taken back to prison at any time for violating the term(s) of his parole.

At some institutions, inmates are called by their surnames, and correctional officers are called "sir." But at Westmorland Institution, it is very informal. Everyone—from inmates to correctional officers to parole officers to teachers to program officers to receptionists to administrative assistants, right on up to the warden—is called by his or her first name.

In my class, the students would either call me "Rosemary" or "Miss." The students from Newfoundland and Labrador attempted to call me "Missus" or "Dear." This was not disrespectful on their part, as it was their custom in Newfoundland. I told them either "Missus, Miss, or Rosemary" was fine, but they should avoid calling me and other women who worked at the institution "Dear." This was difficult for some of them, just because they were so used to saying it and thought it to be respectful. Eventually, though, they were able, with great effort, to avoid saying it.

In particular, one student, Ed, really struggled with this. He would be talking to me, and throughout our conversation I would hear something like, "De— Missus, could I have test number three for math, please?"

Once given the test, he would say, "Thanks, De— Missus."

Ed was very respectful in the classroom, but calling women "Dear" was ingrained in him.

"You gots to be patient with me, Missus. I'm 52 years old, and me ma'am taught me to be calling women 'Dear' or 'Missus'. It's a hard habit to break, but me ma'am also taught me to do as me teacher says."

His pronunciation and grammar were a little difficult to follow at times, but he was a colorful speaker. He was also a student who tried his best to follow the rules and to succeed in class. It really was a pleasure to work with him.

With Ed and the other Newfoundland students, I reassured them that I knew they were not being disrespectful when using "Dear," but I also reinforced that within other parts of the institution and places outside of the province, other women may misinterpret their intended respect as condescension or sarcasm. I told them that we would all work together at breaking the habit. When Newfoundlanders would talk about women they interacted with, such as another teacher, their parole officer, or a random receptionist at the institution, they would say, "The Missus told me ..." or "The Missus in the literacy class ...," meaning the literacy teacher. "Missus" is generally a Newfoundland term as well, but it is totally acceptable.

When inmates came from higher security, it took them a while to get comfortable with the first-name basis. I found that even correctional officers, who had worked at higher security and then came to work at Westmorland Institution, initially struggled with calling inmates by their first names, as well as being called by their first names by the inmates.

I liked the informality at Westmorland Institution. In the classroom, it was easier to set up a teacher-student rapport right from the beginning. I think most people want to be called by their name.

CHAPTER 4

Daily Activities

We had three classrooms in operation at Westmorland Institution. The literacy class was for students working at the grades one through six levels, inclusively. The level two class was for students working on grades seven and eight English, math, and science. The level two class also served all the French students at every level. The level three General Educational Development class served students working towards their GED certificate.

The GED certificate is somewhat equivalent to a high-school diploma. It tests five levels of competency: math, reading skills, science, social studies, and writing. The examinee must pass all subject areas to receive a certificate. If the examinee does not successfully complete all five subject areas, he is not required to rewrite the tests that he successfully completed— he just has to rewrite the tests he did not pass. The GED certificate is also a prerequisite for further education, such as community college, some trade schools, etc. The level three class also provided instruction in all subject areas for those who completed their GED but needed an extra high-school level course in order to be accepted into community college or other academic programs.

Each class accommodated 12 students in the morning and 12 in the afternoon. Some students attended school all day, while others attended either the morning or the afternoon session. We operated on a continuous intake basis. If a classroom had no vacancy, the student was placed on the wait list until a space became available. When students completed a level and were ready to move to the next one, they were advanced immediately, even if the next level had a wait list. Even if there was crowding for a little while, they were given priority and not made to wait for the next available seat. When incarcerated in Canada, as explained in Chapter 2, inmates who do not have a high-school diploma or a GED certificate almost always have school on their case plan in accordance with CD 720. Believing that education is the foundation for making good choices in life and expanding thought processes, school was seen—at that time by CSC—as one of the important ways to rehabilitate inmates in preparation for re-entry into the community.

As teachers, we noted that inmates attending school not only improved academically but also socially. School certainly had a positive effect on all of those who willingly attended from the start. It also had a good effect on those who, at first, grudgingly came to school. I can't say that everyone who came under duress eventually reaped good benefits from attendance, but many of them did.

We tried to maintain the class size at 12, but students came and went. Some students were with us for as little as one to three months. Other students would be there for as long as a couple of years, depending on how long their sentence was and how difficult they found the academic work. Some really struggled but made a great effort to learn. Some were quite bright but put forth little to no effort at all. We had a wide range of remedial work to do.

New students arrived at their work sites, in programs, or in school on Mondays, so Monday mornings were busy for all of us teachers. In addition to supervising and working with our existing class, we needed to orient our new students. On the previous Thursday, we always got notified of how many students we would receive; we would review their academic levels and get their supplies ready for Monday.

Some students would arrive in class with a hopeful attitude, looking forward to catching up on the education that they had missed out on for one reason or another. Other students would arrive reluctantly, thinking of this class as a continuation of past failures and frustration. I would greet students with a smile and try to make them feel comfortable right from the first. I always welcomed new students in a positive way, encouraging them to trust me.

To my students, I would say, "In spite of past difficulties, if we work together as a team, I can guarantee good results."

And I would hold the image of their distraught looks in my mind. Then, once they would start succeeding, I would compare their distraught looks to their new looks of pride and achievement. It was a rewarding experience for both student and teacher: me.

Over my many years of teaching, I had developed a teaching philosophy. For me, this philosophy was simple. It was the responsibility of the teacher for the students' initial learning.

Most children learn in classrooms where the teacher stands in front of the class and teaches to the majority. Along the way, when children get left behind, I believe it is the teacher's responsibility to find out *why* they are left behind. It is also the teacher's responsibility to remediate the problem. If someone cannot learn in the mainstream, a solution must be found by using a different method or a different approach. It is also helpful to determine the student's learning style. This may take time and a lot of effort, but once the teacher is able to teach to that learning style, the learner is able to make great strides. Leaving the learner behind is not an option.

This philosophy may have been a bit easier to achieve in the prison setting due to smaller class sizes and due to the fact that we had a captive audience—no pun intended. However, it still took effort and concentration on both the part of teacher and student. It also required a degree of trust, which had to be built up over time.

CHAPTER 5

One Scary Morning

New students arrived in class on Monday mornings, and on one particular Monday, I had three newcomers. I took them aside, explained the Three Rs to them, assigned them to their desks, gave them their enrollment sheets to fill out, and handed them their required books. Two of the three students sat at their desks and started looking through their books.

But the third one, Tom, walked over to me and said, "Miss, I don't want to be here."

"You don't want to be at this prison?" I asked.

"No, I don't want to be at school" he said.

"Okay, you're assigned to me, so you will have to stay in class for the morning. I will speak to your parole officer at noon, and he will decide if you stay in school or not. I can't speak to him this morning because he is in the Monday morning security briefing until lunchtime. So, please go to your seat, have a look at the books, fill out the form I gave you, and just bide your time. Morning session is over at 11:30," I said.

He did as I directed.

At 9:30 a.m., all of the students left the classroom for a 15-minute smoke break, except for Tom. (Smoking was allowed outside at that time. Since 2008, smoking is not allowed on the premises of federal prisons.) Tom's desk was in the last row at the back of the room. Suddenly, he got up from his desk and started walking towards me. As he neared, he was getting angrier and angrier. His fists were clenched at his sides, and his face was as red as a beet. His walk got heavier and heavier as he approached me.

I kept backing up, unable to reach the door before he got to me. Finally, I couldn't back up any more.

My back was against the wall. My heart was beating so fast and so loud that I thought he would hear it. He stopped right in front of me, right in my face, never mind my personal space.

"Do you know why I got kicked out of public school?" Without waiting for an answer, he yelled, "It was because I took the teacher by the throat."

As scared as I was, I said very calmly, "Tom, I'm hearing that maybe school is not the right place for you. You go over to your unit right now. When I talk to your parole officer, I will make sure that you don't have to attend school."

It was amazing what happened at that exact moment. The red went out of his face. He unclenched his fists, looked at me, smiled, and said, "Thank you, Miss. Have a good day."

And he left.

As per our protocol, I phoned security and reported the incident, which I also had to write up in an incident report. Within the hour, Tom was transported back to a higher-security prison.

Upon reflection, I felt disappointed that I wouldn't get the opportunity to work with this student, who clearly did not have anything good to say about formal education. Sadly, neither of us would get the chance to turn that around. This particular student never returned to Westmorland Institution while I was working there.

It was unusual, but not unheard of, for newcomers to arrive at Westmorland Institution and not be ready for minimum security. Then, after one or two days, they would return to medium security. Most of them would try again after several months. In Tom's case, he must have never reached the minimum-security status.

All staff working in Canadian prisons are trained in dynamic security, with emphasis on being alert and avoiding security incidents when possible. Another important factor is watching out for colleagues. I knew that if I had yelled for help, several staff would have come to my assistance. I would have yelled if diffusing the situation had been unsuccessful. But I sensed that Tom did not have a problem with me personally, but rather his problem was that he feared the classroom setting.

Thankfully, I was able to calm Tom down enough that he was able to walk away. No staff member wants to be the one who has to call for help. Some inmates would view that as a weakness on the part of the staff member and a challenge to see if they were also able to intimidate a staff member into calling for help. In addition to being a nuisance, it would also take valuable time away from teaching.

I am happy to say that in my 25 years of teaching in a federal minimum-security prison for men that was the one and only time I felt afraid or threatened by an inmate.

CHAPTER 6

An Unusual Occurrence

One Tuesday morning in the mid-90s, one of the parole officers, Sandy Ross, walked over to the school to talk to us—the three teachers. He found Pam Oulton, the GED teacher, and Kim Hendrickson, the literacy teacher, in the staff room. Pam came to my class to get me, but when she saw that I was working one-to-one with a student, she didn't disturb us. Later, she and Kim couldn't wait to tell me what was happening.

Sandy was going to have Matt, an inmate who was in the final stages of transitioning into a man, added to his caseload. Matt would arrive on Thursday. Sandy wanted staff to be aware of the situation, but everyone wanted to keep this information from the inmates. He said that Matt would be in the GED class. I was relieved that I would not be dealing with him. My group of students—with arrested development at the middle school or junior high-school level—was the most intolerant, the most judgmental, and the most likely to cause problems if Matt's circumstances were revealed. I was relieved that I wouldn't need to be concerned.

Sandy's, front-end legwork was an example of how well Westmorland Institution worked as far as cooperation among different departments. Everyone involved with an inmate was informed of irregularities and special circumstances right from the beginning so that we were all on the same page. It was highly informative and easier in the long run. It really did pre-empt possible problems down the road.

As it turned out, the Canadian Adult Achievement Test (CAAT) indicated that Matt had a Grade 7 math level and a Grade 8 vocabulary and reading comprehension level. That meant that he would be in my class.

When he arrived, he quickly settled into class. He had a great sense of humor, and it was fun working with him. He would complete a test, put it on my desk, and then two minutes later, he would ask when he could get the results. I always corrected the tests from the bottom of the pile up, from the first to arrive to the last. But he was so persistent in wanting his results that I told him he would get them no later than June 5. At the time it was mid-September, and this became a classroom joke. Whenever anybody wanted anything, someone would say, "Rosemary will have it for you no later than June 5."

Matt completed level two and went on to the GED class. He completed the work for that class and achieved his GED certificate before being paroled. I was glad that he started out in my class. It would have been my loss to have missed out on knowing him. This was yet another lesson on not judging someone before meeting and interacting with him.

Several years later, Matt called me at the institution, asking for a copy of his GED certificate, which he had misplaced. He needed it for a job application. At that time, he told me that he was doing well, had successfully completed all his surgeries, was happy with his life, and thankful for having achieved his GED when he did. He said it had helped him a lot over the years when applying for work.

It is always so good to hear that our former students are doing well. It is rare to hear back from them once they are released back to the community. If they do not return to the institution on a parole violation or for another crime, we just take it for granted that they are doing well.

CHAPTER 7

Snow Sculptures

Living in Eastern Canada, we get quite a bit of snow. We seem to get a lot less than we used to get, although the northern part of New Brunswick still seems to get more than its fair share. Back in the mid-90s, we got a lot of snow from January through to mid-to-late April. One winter at work, both staff and inmates were in a funk due to the cold, never-ending snowy weather. So, I suggested to the other teachers that we try to spark some school spirit by holding a winter carnival, complete with snow games and a snow sculpture competition. The teachers agreed, and we explained to the inmates that there would be a friendly competition among the three classes. Each class would participate as one team competing against the other two classes in various activities planned by us—the teachers. We organized a game of snow Frisbee, a three-legged race, and a snow relay race.

Also, each class had to decide on a sculpture and work together to design and build it. The literacy class built a pool table and used food coloring to make the pool balls. Both the GED class and my level two class had Inuit students. The three Inuit students in my class suggested building an authentic igloo, which the rest of the class approved. The GED class built a polar bear. All of the sculptures were very well done, and the day was a great success.

The three judges, who were staff from the main building, awarded the igloo first place. My class was very excited about this. Isaac, one of the Inuit students and the leader of the project, asked if I had ever been inside an igloo. I hadn't been and accepted his invitation to try it out. I had to crawl through the igloo's extended opening to get inside. Once inside, I could not hear anything happening outside. The other teachers, Pam and Kim, told me that they were shouting questions at me from outside, but I did not respond.

I did not respond because I was in a soundproof room.

It was amazing how warm it was inside the igloo. If I stayed inside for any longer, I would have had to take off my jacket. I am really glad that I tried it. It was one of those moments you need to experience for yourself—not something you can fully grasp just by being told about it.

Although I strongly encouraged Pam and Kim to try it, they both chose not to. So, we finished off the day with hot chocolate, and it seemed to lift the spirits of both the inmates and staff. Several staff from the main building came over to the school to view the sculptures, and they were duly impressed. I do not know if any of them entered the igloo.

When we returned to regular classes and work on Monday, everyone was in better spirits and more prepared to work. A bit of leisure and camaraderie proved to be a good thing. We continued the winter carnival in the school for the next few years. After that, we found we just didn't have enough snow to be able to continue. Global warming?

With the success of the winter activities, we realized that, every once in a while, it would be good to pit the classes against each other in a friendly way. We noticed how much the students within each class pulled together to try to win. They were willing to put their differences aside to try to win the title for their own class. In doing so, we also noticed that there was a lot of planning and a lot of laughing. It was rewarding to see how much the inmates appreciated that we—the teachers—worked hard at setting up the activities for them, and they tried to show their appreciation through good participation.

On these days, we did not observe any hard feelings towards the winners. Everyone seemed to be good-natured and happy to compete. As teachers, we emphasized that the day was meant to have fun. Although there was a winning class for the snow sculpture, there were no losers. Everyone, including the teachers, was getting a day off from working in the classroom. So, we were all winners!

I know that some people reading this will be incensed that we were even trying to have fun days to get inmates out of a winter funk.

I can hear them now:

"Inmates are not supposed to have fun. They are serving time, and it should be somewhat painful."

As I mentioned before, at that time CSC's mandate was to rehabilitate. As part of the team, we would try our best to mold these men into responsible, productive, law-abiding citizens. For those of you who wish for inmates to put in painful hours, days, weeks, months, and possibly years, trust me, you get your wish.

Just being away from their families serves up all the pain possible for these men. Separation from their loved ones is as painful for them as it would be for any one of us. I spent numerous hours in my office with many a student missing his loved ones. When a male inmate becomes emotional to the point of tears in front of his female teacher, you know that his pain and suffering are genuine.

In spite of what the general public may think, these men care very deeply for their wives, children, parents, etc. When a man enters prison, his life gets put on hold, but there is a ripple effect as the lives of all those he touches are put on hold as well.

These men are in prison *as* punishment, not *for* punishment. This means that they are in prison for having broken the law and must atone, but they are not in prison for punishment at the hands of the staff. We were not authorized to try to make their lives more miserable.

Another thing that the general public may be unaware of is that a lot of these men do not know how to have fun. In trying to produce well-rounded students, we thought that teaching fun by example, where the teachers also took part, was just another aspect that would enhance the curriculum.

CHAPTER 8

Spring 2000: Towards Reintegration

Leading up to the year 2000, CSC planned a huge international education conference with both Canada and the United States hosting. The aim of the conference was to welcome as many teachers from as many institutions worldwide as possible. Together, we would share "best practices" and exchange ideas for better ways to implement learning in our classrooms.

The conference took place in Ottawa in the spring of 2000 and was titled Towards Reintegration. Each institution could send as many teachers as they wanted to the conference. CSC would pay to fly one teacher from each institution to Ottawa. Any teacher who wanted to attend was able to, but only one teacher per institution would have their trip paid for by CSC.

Gisele Smith, who was the assistant warden of correctional programs at the time, asked us if we wanted to attend. At Westmorland Institution, there were three teachers. Scott Jardine, the literacy teacher, and I, the level two teacher, were keen to go. Since the GED teacher, Pam Oulton, was going away on a trip with her husband during that time, she was unable to attend. Gisele could have flown there and met us, but she figured that both Scott and I could attend at CSC's expense if we all drove. So, Gisele commissioned an institutional van, and she drove us to the conference. Other passengers in the van were my brother, Rick McAtee—a reading consultant who was presenting at the conference—and Marla Kavalak, regional project manager of the Education Portfolio. (This position was in charge of education for all of the Atlantic prisons.)

Rick had been to Westmorland Institution several times, where he and I put on a number of workshops for the inmates and teachers, as well as the teachers from other institutions.

On the 10-hour trip to Ottawa, we ran into a blizzard in northern New Brunswick—despite it being early May—and almost had to turn back. Gisele was driving. At one point, she hoped that she was not driving too close to a ditch, but she was uncertain because the road was covered in snow and no lines were visible. It was a bit scary for a few minutes. Then, almost as suddenly as the storm emerged, we quickly drove out of it. The rest of the way was clear, and Gisele did not have any other driving problems.

While Gisele drove, Marla rode shotgun. Scott sat in the middle seat and alternately chatted and slept. Rick and I sat in the furthest back seat of the van. Along the way, Rick and I wrote in our notepads, and we discussed different ways to get students to take more responsibility for their own learning. Since Rick is a reading consultant, we were trying to figure out ways to make reading more fun and easier to accomplish.

At one point during the car ride, Gisele and Marla turned to us and said, "Are you two working back there?"

"No, we're talking about facilitating reading in the classroom," I said.

"That's working!" they both said at once.

The truth is that even when we are on vacation at the family camp in Maine, Rick and I are usually talking about some aspect of teaching. It is just in us both—teachers are who we are and teaching is what we do.

During our talks in the back of that van, Rick and I came up with an idea. Rick believed students could improve their reading comprehension and vocabulary if they read books below their reading level. The students would need to read aloud to perfection. He suggested that they read children's books.

"No, I am not asking inmates to read children's books aloud. They would be insulted and shut down on me. I could lose them," I said to Rick.

Rick said that we should devise a legitimate reason for inmates to read children's books. So, we decided that we would operate a project in the school at Westmorland Institution, where the inmates would read children's books and record them onto cassette tapes. Our idea was that if this worked, we would get permission to send the books and tapes out to the public schools for children to learn from the inmates' work. I could hardly wait to get back to the institution to get this project on the go!

When we returned to Westmorland Institution, Rick and I started encouraging students to join our project. Our hypothesis was: "If a student reads aloud to fluency, he will improve his comprehension and vocabulary skills without any extra effort on the part of the learner or the teacher." We had researched this and did not find any studies that confirmed this to be true.

We set out to prove or disprove our theory.

At the time, I had a student in my class, Peter, who seemed to be a leader but not always in a good way. He was sometimes disdainful of institutional or school rules and voiced his opinion quite openly and loudly. He was a *tough guy*. Because the other inmates looked up to him, they would not disagree with him. Sometimes this slowed down their ability to make progress.

I thought our project would give Peter an opportunity to lead in a positive and productive manner and would encourage him to use his influence appropriately. I approached him, explained what we planned to do, and asked him if he would help us get our project under way. But Peter flatly refused. He said it was a babyish project and he wanted nothing to do with it. I accepted his refusal and began looking for someone else.

Two days later, seemingly under duress, Peter approached me and grudgingly said he would join. Wondering why he would agree when he clearly seemed defensive about the whole thing, I did not question but wholeheartedly welcomed him and thanked him for coming on board. I only found out later that Rick had talked to him and played the *grateful* card:

"Hasn't Rosemary done many things to help you, Peter? Don't you want to thank her?"

Peter asked me what he should do next. I gave him four or five children's books and asked him to practice reading them aloud. I told him he needed to read them perfectly, without any mistakes.

"Rosemary, you want too much. I'm an inmate. I'm going to make mistakes," he said.

I told him that if we sent cassette tapes with mistakes to the elementary schools, then children would end up making the same mistakes. What good would the children get out of that?

"You want perfect? I'll give you perfect," he said after thinking about it for a few seconds.

"Thank you."

Peter got to work. He took it very seriously, and it was thanks to him that our project quickly got off the ground. He helped recruit other students, and we got underway, preparing books and cassette tapes for the elementary school children.

The project took off! Peter became my number one go-to person. He coached other students in reading to perfection. He assisted others with recording their reading onto cassette tapes, and he checked the quality of all recordings before passing them on to me for the final check. By this time, he had really bought into the project, and he was proud of it and of his work.

Staff at the institution started noticing students walking around with children's books under their arms, and sometimes in front of their faces. So, one day, one of the correctional officers in the main control center phoned me.

"Rosemary, you must caution the inmates not to walk along the pathways to their units while reading. Someone is going to trip and fall," he said.

I heeded the advice from the control center, and I told the inmates to be careful and not to read while walking. Then, I basked in the pleasure of knowing that these non-readers were now reading all the time.

A few days later, Peter's parole officer called and said that when Peter met with her, he pulled out his book and asked if he could read it to her. She was surprised, but agreed.

When he got to the part in the story that said, "Chomp, chomp, chomp," she laughed aloud. Peter did not appreciate her laughter.

"What are you doing? I'm trying to achieve perfection for the children. This is a serious project. You are supposed to tell me if I make a mistake, not laugh at me," Peter said to her.

She said she was sorry, and he finished the book. As soon as he was out of her office, she phoned me.

"What's going on with the reading? I didn't know about a project. You should inform all staff, so they don't make the same mistake I just made," the parole officer said to me.

I thought this was great and really attested to Peter's level of commitment.

I sent out a memo to all staff informing them of our project. I explained that each reader was to read his book aloud to three different people before attempting to record it onto a cassette tape. I spoke to the students who were participating and suggested that maybe parole officers were too busy to listen to them read.

"But we need three people to listen. Where do we find them?" one student asked.

"Each one of you lives with five others. Can't one of them listen to you?" I asked.

"Oh! Inmates can listen, too?" they asked.

"Well, inmates are people, aren't they?"

We all had a laugh about that, and productivity continued.

One day, we had several readers recording onto cassette tapes, when Peter alerted me to a problem. The recorder was picking up a lot of outside noise. Despite the reader reading perfectly, noises from construction, bells, the intercom, and people talking could be heard in the background. We asked to have a booth made where sounds could not travel inside. Once it was built, we placed it in one of the classrooms that we had taken over as the Westmorland Literacy Project room. It worked well, and the guys found it to be fun.

For low-level books —for children in kindergarten through grade two—the reader would read the book and record it on both sides of the tape. On one side of the tape, he would ring a bell at the end of each page indicating that the listener should turn the page.

Weeks after I had sent out the memo to staff explaining our project, one of my readers, George, told me he had been reading to a staff member every morning at 10 a.m.

But one morning, George had not shown up to read. Over the intercom, George heard,

"George, it's 10 o'clock. I'm waiting."

"He thinks I should be there every morning to read to him," George said to me.

"Is that a problem?" I asked.

George paused for a couple of seconds. "No," he said.

"Well, then go read, and have fun!" I advised.

The next day, another staff member saw George leaving the office next door and said, "How come nobody comes to read to me?"

So, George started reading to him, too.

It was amazing to see how much the staff responded to this project. Mike Corbett, Westmorland Institution's warden, was so supportive that he made it easier for us to accomplish many of our goals by being willing to provide us whatever we needed. We owed him a great deal of gratitude. Everyone, from the top down, knew about the project and wholeheartedly supported us.

Here are some comments about the reading project.

From our inmate readers:

"Angie helped me with some of the words, such as 'phosphorescent,' 'sextant,' 'luminous,' etc." —*George*

"Rose, you have created monsters … this is all we want to do … read." —*Peter*

"I love this *Pigs Aplenty* book so much. I don't want to tape it because then I'll be done with it." —*Greg*

"I'm not sure I can read these long, hard books, but I'll give them a try." —*Glen*

"The most important thing is that the readers feel good about themselves and the project." —*Joe, reading tutor*

From staff:

"Come on in, George, I'm ready for my story." —*Staff member, wanting to help*

"Why am I left out? I like to hear bedtime stories, too. Why has nobody come to read to me?" —*Another staff member*

"I think his aural comprehension has improved a great deal as well." —*Mary King, teacher, referring to her level one student (Aural comprehension is the gradual improvement of the student's ability to understand language in its spoken form.)*

"I can't believe that guy on my caseload is reading so well. I thought he was almost illiterate." —*Mario Comeau, parole officer, referring to a level one student who was illiterate before coming to school and joining the reading program*

"I'm amazed that macho, criminal types will sit and read these books, inserting sound effects, like 'chomp, chomp, chomp,' and not laugh or bat an eye. They really take this project seriously." —*Anita Silliker, parole officer, regarding readers practicing in her office*

CHAPTER 9

Ready for the Public-School Teachers: Introducing the Westmorland Literacy Project

After having the inmates work on the cassette tapes for several months—five months to be exact—Rick and I both believed we were ready to introduce our reading project to the teachers from the public-school district. We were ready to ask for permission from the warden to offer our product to the public schools. We met first with Dan Smyth, assistant warden of correctional programs. Right from the start, he was aware that we were working to improve literacy in the school.

Dan also knew that Mike, our warden, had made a commitment to Alphonse Cormier, the regional deputy commissioner, regarding reintegration initiatives and community outreach. Dan spoke to Mike about this project, and, in turn, Dan arranged for me to speak to him.

The warden wanted us to meet with some school officials before starting to send out the books to the teachers. He and I had a meeting in his office with Eric Peters and Terry King, both early years supervisors for School District 2.

We showed them our packaged books. Each package contained four books of the same title, a cassette taped on both sides (one side of the cassette tape included a prompting bell each time the inmate completed reading a page), and an order form where the teachers could pick next month's books. Our plan was that each teacher would receive three of these packages on a lending basis for a period of one month. We would not dictate how the teacher would use these materials. But we suggested they could sit four children at a learning center to listen to the cassette, and each child would have their own book to track the speaker's voice. We recommended this because it had been proven that reading to someone is more effective if the listener sees the script being read.

While explaining the packages, I noticed Terry mouthing to Eric that each package would be worth about $10.00. He was right. If we had needed to pay for the books with each one at a minimum of $6.00, and a cassette tape at a minimum of $2.00, a plastic envelope at $1.75, the cost of a package would be a minimum total of $9.75, not counting time and effort to tape a good product. (Rick had provided us with the children's books for our start-up. Westmorland Institution, through Mike, provided everything else: the cassette tapes, the envelopes, the index cards for the book titles, etc.)

Since we were in the warden's office in a federal prison, Eric finally brought up the subject that we had anticipated. He asked me if I had any sex offenders working on the project. I told him that I had several. He then asked me if I would let a sex offender read to my children. I said I would not, but I would allow my children to listen to one reading on a cassette tape, especially if I knew the tape would be quality controlled by me or someone I trusted. People that I trusted to do this were not inmates, although by the time the inmate in charge delivered the finished product to me, it was usually mistake-free. I then explained that no offender of any crime would ever be in direct contact with any children.

With that out of the way, Eric and Terry wholeheartedly came on board, believing that teachers would love this project and that both teachers and children would benefit from it.

We set up an evening to welcome teachers and invite them to borrow books. We held the event in the early evening of November 21, 2000, in the basement of Immaculate Heart of Mary Church in Riverview, New Brunswick. We had good attendance. Rick was there, and he spoke about our efforts since the Ottawa conference. Our warden addressed the crowd and Jean Guy Bourque, CSC's regional manager of correctional programs, spoke to the group.

We also brought three inmates to this event. They were all readers who worked to benefit the children. They each read an excerpt from one of the books they had taped. One of the inmates, Curt, was a bit hesitant about reading in front of a group, never mind a group of teachers. I told him that there was no pressure and it was okay if he decided not to read. Secretly, I thought it would be really good for him to read since it would boost his confidence. But I knew him well enough to know that if I pushed him, he would not do it for sure.

When it was Curt's turn, he nodded to me that he was willing, and I introduced him. He was reading an excerpt from *Borreguita and the Coyote* by Verna Aardema. When he got to the place where the coyote howled out in pain, Curt put his head back and did the most fantastic coyote howl I ever heard. The crowd was still for a second and then erupted in applause. At the end of the evening, when the teachers could come forward and pick the packages they wanted to take to their classrooms for the month, all of the teachers wanted *Borreguita and the Coyote*. We had to make a wait list for that title. To say that this was a giant boost to Curt's confidence would be an understatement.

Before joining the project, Curt had been an unwilling student. He continually arrived late, wasn't very motivated, and didn't accomplish much work throughout the day. One rule for joining the reading project was that students had to stay on top of their classroom work. Reading and recording onto cassette tapes was done during school time, but students were not free to spend all of their time doing that.

Once Curt started working on the reading project, a subtle change came over him. He became a more dedicated and more willing student. His howl at the presentation set the tone for him to believe in himself and to consider working towards his GED. Before that, he didn't think he was up to the task and preferred to pretend that he didn't want or need further education. His new-found confidence gave him the impetus to complete the level two class, advance to the GED class, and eventually obtain his GED certificate, succeeding in all five subject areas on his first try.

As we explained our book packaging system to the teachers, just as we had to the early years supervisors, Eric and Terry, in the warden's office, the teachers loved that they could order the titles they wanted in advance. That meant that they could order reading materials based on their students' learning outcomes. The books would be boxed by Westmorland Institution and delivered by our prison's driver to the School District 2's board office, where the packages would be distributed to the individual schools. At the end of the month, our driver would collect the boxes to return to us, and we would complete a "turnaround," where my workers would inventory the returned books, sort the requests, and send the boxes back for the next month.

I scheduled one coordinator—an inmate— Mark, at the time, to direct and quality control the turnaround. (Coordinators changed due to inmates leaving for various reasons, such as parole, programming, work releases, etc. When one would leave, I would hire and train another one.) Since our goal was to have the boxes ready to go back out within two days of receiving them, my coordinator was rushed off his feet during these two days. I very much relied on him to get the job done. He did not disappoint me.

During the rest of his time at Westmorland School, he worked for The Westmorland Literacy Project in whatever capacity we needed. Over the years, I hired several coordinators and, for the most part, they were dedicated, hard-working employees. Whenever I had an opening, I would interview a prospective inmate employee and then ask the work shift board to assign that inmate to me.

In addition to the turnaround coordinator, I hired two reading coaches. The reading coaches were educated inmates who helped me immensely because they prepared the readers to record. One of the coaches would listen to a reader on a one-to-one basis and alert him to any mistakes he was making. Then, when the coach thought the reader was ready, they would venture into the recording booth to make the cassette. This took time, patience, and lots of repetition. When mistakes were made, the reader would have to start all over again. The coaches were very good at knowing when to shut it down with the intention of coming back to it. They guarded against letting readers become frustrated.

It was the repetition that really benefitted the reader as it made him more aware of what he was reading, proving our hypothesis that fluency led to comprehension. Of course, we did not inform the reader that this was the goal. For him, the goal was to present a perfect product for the listening children. My readers took this as a big responsibility, as well as a great honor.

As time went on, we were averaging six or seven turnarounds per school year. In September, we would send our book lists out for requests from the teachers. It would take most of September to register our participating teachers and receive their orders. When the November books were returned to us, we did not turn them around for December. We had learned that December was too busy a month for the teachers and students to use our packages. We waited until January to start sending out our materials again.

From public-school teachers:

"I have a couple of hyperactive students in my Grade 3 class. I have used commercially made tapes, and these students are terrible with those because they use background music. These students focus in on the music and do not hear the story at all. Your tapes are wonderful. They listen attentively to them because there is silence in the background."
—*A teacher from Dorchester Elementary School*

"Thank you for the borrow-a-book program! Thank you to *all* the readers! We loved hearing all the books!"
—*A teacher from Port Elgin Regional School*

CHAPTER 10

Getting to Work

Over the years while working at Westmorland Institution, I carpooled sometimes and drove by myself other times. I am not sure what year it was, but I had been working there for quite a while when Barry said to me, "You should have a cellphone just in case anything happens on the way to or from work."

He got me a cellphone.

The next day, I was driving three passengers, and we were almost at work—about three kilometers away—when the muffler fell off my car. We all got out and looked at the muffler, partially on the road.

"Never fear … I have a cell phone," I said.

I called Barry and told him that the muffler fell off.

"Thanks for telling me. Have a good day." And he hung up.

After a few seconds of looking at the phone in puzzlement, I told the others that we had to figure something out. We rigged up the muffler with one of our ID lanyards, and I drove the rest of the way.

As soon as I got to my office at Westmorland Institution, I phoned the on-site mechanic in charge of the institutional fleet of vans. I asked him if I would be able to drive all the way back to Riverview with the lanyard holding up the muffler. He said he didn't think so because he thought the lanyard would burn off. He advised me to bring my car to the on-site garage, and he would have an inmate fix it up.

After waiting for me to get there, he introduced me to the inmate worker who would take care of it, and then he left to do another job. This inmate told me that, in the community, he was a mechanic, and he asked what happened. I told him; I also told him that I had phoned my husband, but my husband only thanked me for telling him and hung up.

The inmate asked what I had expected him to do.

"I expected him to drop everything and speed to my rescue," I said.

He looked at me. "Yeah, my wife would have expected that, too," he said.

Once the inmate finished the job, I went back to my class and got to work. I was sitting at my desk when I realized that I had brought my cellphone—stored in my book bag—into the school. This was entirely unacceptable and against all rules of security. I rushed down to my office, retrieved my cellphone, and put it in the glove compartment of my car.

It was the early days of cellphones, so even if it was locked up in my office, it was against the rules to bring the cellphone inside. This was a huge inconvenience while carpooling because having to leave my cellphone in another driver's car was a nuisance as it was so easy to forget it there at the end of the day. Today, the rules have been relaxed, and cellphones may be stored in offices now. Anyway, since it was such a difficulty to have at the time, and it didn't get me instant service, I decided I would turn it back over to Barry.

Later that afternoon, the phone in my classroom rang. It was Barry asking if he should come down to Westmorland Institution to pick us up. I asked why he would do that, and he said that he thought we had car trouble. I told him it was fine, and I would see him at home.

Once I got home, he said that he would take the car to have the muffler fixed. But I told him that we were all set. I told him that an inmate had already fixed it. He said he wanted to be sure and took it to a garage in Riverview. He told them what had happened, and they checked it out. They told him they could redo it, but it would not be any better than how it was already done.

One needs to remember that all of the men at the institution are not only inmates. Most of them have lots of good skills, just like anyone in the general population. Barry didn't trust this to be true, but I knew I could trust that it was done well.

CHAPTER 11

Spring 2001:
A Personal Hardship

One morning in the fall of 2000, after showering I noticed a huge protruding lump on my right breast that hadn't been there the night before. During my break at work, I phoned my doctor's office and was given an appointment for the next day. When I saw my doctor, he assured me that it couldn't be anything serious because it appeared too quickly. Four months earlier, I had had a clear mammogram. So, he scheduled me for another mammogram in a month's time. We didn't need to act fast because he suspected it was just fluid. In the meantime, I worked as usual and put it out of my mind.

After I had the mammogram, it came back as suspicious, but again, it was thought to be fluid. My doctor then scheduled me for an MRI to get a clearer picture. After the MRI results came back, which again were inconclusive, my doctor scheduled an appointment with a breast cancer specialist. Again, I was assured this was just a precaution.

I met with the specialist, and he held the same opinion that the lump must be fluid. But he said he didn't know for sure what it was—he just knew that it should not be there. He scheduled me for a biopsy the next week to remove it and have it tested. After the biopsy, I was given an appointment to see him two weeks later.

The Thursday following the surgery, I got a call from the specialist's receptionist asking me to attend an appointment with him the next day—and to bring my husband with me. Now I knew, in spite of all the assurances, that I had something serious.

By this point, it was April 2001.

Barry and I went to the appointment the next day and found that I had stage 2 breast cancer. The doctor was very nice and calmly told me my options. After careful conversation with him, I decided to have another surgery to try to remove all of the affected matter. After that, I expected to undergo chemotherapy and radiation treatments.

The good news is that all of the cancer was removed and the margins were clear. I had two weeks off from work to recover from this surgery. Two days after the surgery, I was resting in bed and opened my eyes to see my daughter, Aimée, looking at me. I knew this was impossible because Aimée lived in Tucson, Arizona. I closed my eyes and when I opened them again, she was still there. Rick, my brother, had sent her home to spend a few days with me. When she left to go back to Arizona, my other daughter, Alicia, had just finished university for the summer and I got to spend the rest of my recovery with her. My three sons were all nearby; Joe and his wife, Heather, living a few blocks away, and Jon and Jeff, both at home. Barry and all of them were very attentive.

The specialist had told me that women who had good family support tended to heal faster and had a better prognosis than women who were on their own. I certainly had the best support system possible. When I went back for a checkup, I had healed well. Because the doctor believed that the cancer was hormone-related, he had decided that I didn't need chemotherapy but only 20 radiation treatments.

Now, putting this in relation to work, I spoke to Dan Smyth, the assistant warden of correctional programs—and told him that I would like to work while having the radiation treatments, if possible. I had managed to get the last appointment of the day, at 3:30 p.m. from Monday to Friday, at the Georges Dumont Hospital in Moncton. Dan was so generous in allowing me to shut down my class at 2:50 p.m., rather than 4 p.m. each day for a month in order to attend these appointments.

I intended to work with the understanding that if my tolerance was low, I would have to take a small leave of absence and get a substitute teacher.

I attended each of my 20 treatments at 3:30 p.m. and was back in my home in Riverview by 4 p.m. It was summer. Joe and his wife, Heather, lived nearby. And everyone else was home for vacation: Aimée and her husband, Stephen Lockie, from their home in Tucson, Arizona; Alicia from university; and Jon and Jeff, who still lived at home, were on summer vacation from high school and middle school, respectively. There was lots of help. I would come home and lie on the couch while Barry made supper. Sometimes I would doze off, and other times I would just rest. When called to supper, I would get up, eat, do all the usual evening routines, and then go to bed at my usual time. The next day, I would get up and do it all again.

The radiation specialist told me that because I have very fair skin, I could expect quite a bit of discomfort due to burning and itching, but the treatments went off without a hitch. I was not in any discomfort at all. I was not overly tired, and I seemed to heal very well.

After my last treatment, I phoned my mother and told her that I was finished.

"Wow! Those students are going to have a fit, having to stay in class until 4 o'clock now," she said.

"What do you mean those students, Mom? I'm going to have a fit having to stay until 4 o'clock," I said.

I was extremely fortunate that everything went so well for me. I very much appreciate my supervisor, Dan, who made allowances for me and I appreciate all of my co-workers, who picked up the slack as needed. I have told this story to show how considerate the CSC administrators were. It really made me feel like a valued part of the overall Westmorland Institution team. It truly made for great working conditions.

CHAPTER 12

French Students

Canada is a bilingual country. All federal services must be offered in both official languages, English and French. New Brunswick is the only bilingual province. Provincially, services in New Brunswick, by law, must be available in both official languages, English and French.

Quebec is a unilingual French province, and the rest of the provinces are unilingual English provinces.

Westmorland is a federal institution in the bilingual province of New Brunswick. We are required to serve inmates in one of the official languages of their choice.

When I first started working at Westmorland Institution, I had very few French students, although I was the only bilingual teacher and all French students were in my class. I only had one or two here and there. We did have a complete French curriculum, one that I thought was very comprehensive, easy to follow, and a pleasure to teach.

These very few French students would be in class among the English students, but working in their own language and using this French curriculum. This curriculum was an authentic French curriculum, not a translation of an English curriculum. I spoke to my French students exclusively in French. It was amazing how quickly these students learned English from the students around them.

As time went on, we started to have more and more French students and it became a bit more problematic having them dispersed among the English students. I did a bit of research into the Language Act which stated that if one-third of the participants in a class were requesting service in French, then they needed to have their own class. I wrote a proposal requesting to have French students in the mornings and English students in the afternoons. This request was granted and it was so much easier for me and the students. The French students continued to rapidly learn English (not in class), because outside of class, their environment was predominantly English.

Some of my French students were just as reluctant to come to school as the English ones were. One student in particular, Daniel, hated school and this contempt carried over to me. He and I were never on the same page, but I worked with him in the same way I worked with any other student. While I did not allow him to be openly disrespectful towards me, I tolerated his moodiness by ignoring it. I tried to be as pleasant as possible and pretended not to notice how grumpy he always was.

Daniel needed to work on Grade 8 math before taking on the GED work. Once he had completed the math, I gave him the pre-tests for GED and he scored quite well. In spite of his distaste for school, he was quite bright. I used his good scores to try to encourage him. He said he did not care. He said he did not need his GED certificate and did not even want it. He was only in school to satisfy his parole officer.

When I thought he was ready, I scheduled a GED writing. Unlike when I first started working at Westmorland Institution, the students no longer went out to Moncton Community College or, in this case, to the Dieppe Community College (French) to be tested. About every two months, we had an examiner employed by the province to come in to the institution and administer the tests.

Daniel wrote the five tests and when the results came back, they were in a large brown envelope. GED results that arrive in a white business envelope indicate that the examinee did not pass all five subject areas. Results that come in a large brown envelope contain the marks as well as the 8-by-10 certificate. So, I knew that Daniel had passed before opening it.

When I gave Daniel his results and his certificate, he was extremely pleased. He told me I was the best teacher in the world. He was so happy, he asked to leave the school area for a few minutes. He ran to his parole officer's office and told him the "great news." He told anyone who would listen that school was what it was all about. He said that getting your GED is the most important thing you can do while incarcerated. Nobody was more surprised by his reaction than I was. He went from disdainful to exuberant. It was really great to see.

Another surprising thing was that Daniel opted to stay in school to work on advanced math. Once he received his GED certificate, he would have been allowed to leave school and go to work somewhere in the institution. It seemed that his whole attitude and demeanor towards school changed once he had obtained his certificate. He was not as moody, he smiled more than he ever had before, and he promoted school to new students and encouraged them to do their best.

I really enjoyed teaching French in the mornings and English in the afternoons. It allowed me to be fully present for each group, rather than having to divide my attention between the two. It also was a great way for me to keep up and even improve my French-language skills. It is very easy to lose a second language when you rarely use it.

CHAPTER 13

Meeting Mr. Dick Robinson

In July of 2002, my mom and Rick joined my youngest son, Jeff, and me on a trip to New York City for a few days. Jeff felt he needed to visit Ground Zero after the 9/11 tragedy in 2001. Jeff was 14 years old at the time.

For years, Rick had worked for Scholastic Books as a freelance reading consultant. So, he booked an appointment for us to meet with Mr. Dick Robinson, the owner of Scholastic Books. We were set to tell him about our success at Westmorland Institution, where we were continuing our reading project and were very successful in liaising with the public-school system.

We had a 2 p.m. appointment, and Rick and I arrived at 1:45 p.m. Rick had told me that Mr. Robinson was a very busy man, and we had been blocked into his schedule for half an hour. Rick cautioned me not to get carried away with anecdotes and stories about the program but to stick to answering Mr. Robinson's questions concisely and to the point. When we met with him, he did not seem hurried in the least. He is a charming, congenial man, and he was very easy to talk to. He asked me several questions about my project.

I was answering as succinctly as possible, yet he was eager to learn more.

"But Rosemary, I want to know how the inmates feel about the project. I want to know how the public-school teachers and students feel about the project. Is there joy in what is being worked on? Are the students enhanced by the inmates' work? Are the inmates happy?" Mr. Robinson asked.

I glanced at Rick, and with a small nod to him, I indicated that I was interpreting Mr. Robinson's questions as the go-ahead for storytelling and sharing. I told Mr. Robinson how the inmate students felt like worthwhile contributors and how their behavior had changed for the better because they wanted to be part of helping children.

Before ending the meeting, Mr. Robinson asked what he could do to help. Rick asked if Scholastic Books could provide 50 titles with five copies per title—a total of 250 free books. Without batting an eye, Mr. Robinson granted it to us. He also offered us a program entitled READ 180. This program was worth several thousand dollars. Up to this point, we had not been relying on additional instruction because our hypothesis was that reading comprehension would improve without any extra effort on the part of the teacher or the student. Mr. Robinson thought it would be interesting to see how much more improvement could be made with extra instructional materials.

He offered the READ 180 program to me on the condition that I would use it at Westmorland Institution as it was written and intended. Also, he wanted me to gather data through pre- and post-testing and to submit my results to him after running the program for 10 weeks. Certainly, I agreed. Teachers are always excited to get new innovative materials.

We left the meeting at 3:45 p.m., thinking that half hour had flown by! And we were impressed with Mr. Robinson's generosity as he made us feel at home.

We also made an agreement with Mr. Robinson. He gave us permission to use and record the books he sent us. In return, we agreed not to sell or give the books away. The books were to be used as learning tools for both our inmates and for the public-school teachers and students. We would not get any monetary benefit from any of the materials. This was a fine deal for us because it gave us very extensive resources to use in order to prove or disprove our hypothesis.

For the READ 180 program, every participant completed a reading test from Scholastic called the Scholastic Reading Inventory (SRI). This assessment indicated the reading comprehension level of the examinee. Each participant took this test, even if he was already a good reader. I administered these tests and recorded the results. Our goal was to prove or disprove our hypothesis: "reading lower-level books repeatedly to perfection would improve comprehension." The inmates' goals were to help children and to use their time at the institution in a productive manner. To accomplish our collective goals, we used the SRI to collect quantitative data.

Some inmates were not attempting to improve their reading comprehension skills but wanted to be part of helping out. We did not turn anyone away. Whoever wanted to participate was always welcome. There were several participants who did not attend school but visited during their off-time to take the test, select books, practice, and then record. Some higher-level students eventually requested to become tutors, believing that they could contribute more at school than working on the farm or some other institutional job. This is not to detract from those jobs but to highlight that further education was always a good idea.

We—the teachers—noticed that being affiliated with the reading program and the school setting seemed to put inmates in a more socially acceptable frame of mind. It opened them up to thinking of more effective ways to help children. Working hard to help children left the inmates little time to think of ways to cheat the system or create other deceitful plans. It was a win-win situation—the harder they worked, the less they were interested in wasting time on devious matters.

After the readers recorded for 10 weeks, I would administer the SRI test again. Low-level readers scored the most progress. Some readers advanced two or three grade levels. Since some of the higher-level readers had achieved perfect scores the first time around, they quantitatively did not show progress. How would one score higher than perfect? But some of those readers expressed more confidence in reading aloud and were more willing to speak or read aloud in a group setting. We found that with the reading program, nobody scored lower the second time around.

Therefore, we noted that both from a quantitative and qualitative standpoint, our hypothesis was proven correct.

Now, with Mr. Robinson's READ 180 Program, we were prepared to go to the next level. I was proud to implement these materials at Westmorland Institution. If Mr. Robinson had not provided the materials, I am certain that the institution would not have been willing to pay for them. We were able to offer better learning opportunities than the other institutions. Our warden, Mike Corbett, made it possible for me to take advantage of these materials by providing the school with six high-end computers (two per class) that could accommodate the program. If teachers in other institutions wanted to write grants or ask for donations, they were free to do so.

Mr. Robinson has been a great success throughout his professional career. He is an extremely smart man with tremendous business acumen—I believe his success is related to that, as well as to his generosity and kindness.

Thank you again, Mr. Robinson, for helping me so much with my class at Westmorland Institution.

CHAPTER 14

Implementing READ 180

The READ 180 program consisted of four 20-minute activities, occurring five days a week. The activities included: 20 minutes of class instruction (the teacher would lead this, focusing on a specific topic or grammar-related intervention), 20 minutes of either a group or individual activity (the students would work on a handout sheet previously prepared by the teacher to reinforce the class activity), 20 minutes of the computer READ 180 program (this was a leveled program, which built on success), and 20 minutes of private reading (the students read from the books provided by the program).

It was my top priority to ensure that we adhered to the 20-minute periods to maintain the integrity of the program. I had promised to send data to Mr. Robinson, and I kept my promise. The other teachers used aspects of the program and had success in some areas, but their data was inapplicable since they did not adhere to the timelines and activities presented by the program. So, I did not include the other teachers' results when I sent mine.

Before we started the READ 180 program, we had to make sure the computers were set and ready to accommodate the program. Mr. Robinson sent a technician and a READ 180 teacher, at his expense, from New York City to Westmorland Institution, for two days to work with us and teach us the ins and outs of the program. Our own IT specialist, Nelson Imbeault, joined us and became familiar with all the technology so that he could maintain our computers once Mr. Robinson's team was gone. This was yet another attestation to the kindness and generosity of Mr. Robinson. At the same time, it also attested to the support from our warden in supplying the computers and the services of Nelson for two full days.

The following week, I spent a lot of time sifting through the program during my lunch break before introducing it to my class. I did some preparation work on group and individual activities. My classroom tutors—inmates—created some activities for me based on my specifications. And I bought a plastic utility cart on wheels and made individual file folders for each student.

Finally, I was ready to introduce the READ 180 program to my students. Although they did not have a choice, I wanted to ensure they were on board with me and not reluctantly participating. I told them that a very generous man had given me some learning materials, and together we—the inmates and I—would pilot those materials in class. Then I would send the results to this generous donor. With our results, he would be able to improve these materials for school children, who were learning to read. I stressed that their input would be very valuable for the future of the program.

Most of the students bought into the program right away, while others needed a bit more encouragement. Starting out, I didn't care if they were not excited about it because I knew, in the end, the program would draw them in.

I explained that in the plastic utility cart, there was a file folder for each student with his name on it. I told them that at the end of each day, they would each leave their chosen books in the cart and fill out the enclosed sheet, documenting which page they were on and the part of the story where they had finished for the day. A couple weeks later, everyone was becoming quite adept at following the activities, and I wasn't monitoring them as closely as when we started.

One morning at my desk, I was working with a student on math when I realized that one of the students was still reading.

"Jack, please put that book away. You have been reading for almost an hour."

"Can I just finish this chapter?"

"How many pages?"

He counted the pages. "Six," he said.

"No, that'll take too long. Please, put it away now."

I had denied Jack's request since I had promised Mr. Robinson that I would guard the integrity of the program by sticking to the 20-minute activity time frames.

Jack read while walking across the classroom, took his folder out of the cart, wrote on his sheet, and put his book and folder back in the cart. Later, when the students had gone to lunch, I checked his folder.

On his sheet, he had written with force: "I just wish Rose would let us read."

This was from a student who had been a poor reader and had never read a chapter book to completion. Although I didn't tell Jack, I was thrilled that he and many other poor readers were improving so dramatically that they were becoming avid readers. The enjoyment of reading was starting to be their norm. I couldn't have been happier.

Before being paroled, Jack applied for and was granted a pass to go home for Christmas. During this break at home, he read to his children for the first time. He was confident and felt that he had read well and both he and his children had enjoyed it immensely. When he returned to the institution, he was so happy and proud. He told everyone how rewarding it was to be able to read to his children. Many staff members were very touched to hear his story.

A lot of us take reading for granted and do not consider it a big deal. But it really would be a big deal if you had not been able to read all through your childhood and then were given the opportunity to learn.

Before Jack left the institution on day parole, I told him how impressed I was with his progress and how good a reader he had become. He thanked me for the opportunity to use the resources available and for allowing him to be part of the Westmorland Literacy Project, where he had read 15 books for the children. He also said he was excited to be able to continue to read to his own children—a job he had previously left to their mother.

The computer part of the READ 180 program was a big hit with everyone. The program was set up like a video game where you must accomplish each task before moving on to the next one. The READ 180 tutor, Ty, was so kind and encouraging. He did not make students feel inferior when they made mistakes. He just told them to try again. If they had a particularly difficult session, at the end of their 20 minutes, he would advise them to put it aside and try again tomorrow. I know this because when practicing using the program, I went into it twice as two different students. The first time I didn't make any mistakes and wanted to know if Ty would advance me through the levels because of my perfect score. He did not.

"Wow! You nailed it. Tomorrow you'll do well, starting where you left off," he said.

When I went in as the second student, I got almost everything wrong, and wanted to know what would happen if this were the case for one of my students. I wanted to know what Ty's reaction would be and what the student would have to do to go on from there.

Ty said, "You seem to have had a bit of difficulty today. When you come back tomorrow, we'll work on these same concepts and we'll get through it together."

Then, when I went back, I found that for every mistake I had made, I had to get that same thing correct in three different situations before I could go on to the next thing. The program was excellent. It was laid out in a manner where it appeared that you were doing lots of different activities. As a teacher, I recognized the three different places where I was doing the same thing. Most students would not recognize that, but would be okay with accepting the video-game layout of succeeding at a level before being allowed to go on.

At the time, I had two inmate tutors working with me in the classroom. I suggested to the tutors that they follow the computer program along with the students, despite being beyond the levels included in the program. I wanted the tutors to do this because if the students had questions, the tutors would be able to field them if I were working with someone else. The tutors did not object to completing the computer activities, and they were a big help in the classroom. Sometimes the tutors were helpful without doing much. Just being there and participating was enough to set a good example for my struggling students.

One of the tutors, Connor, said that he got some pointers for tutoring from Ty. He said he learned how to praise without going overboard and he learned how to be encouraging when the student was clearly having a hard time. I was pleased that the tutors were putting so much into it. It really was noted by the students, and since the students really respected the tutors, it put a positive light on the program and on learning itself.

When inmates gave themselves permission to not be the "tough guy," they could learn so much. I tried to keep my classroom as a safe place to learn without the need to save face.

"If you don't know the material, let's make sure you learn it," I would tell my students.

I also made sure that my students understood that they could learn as much or more from their fellow classmates as they could from me. When everyone is working towards the same goal, we all win.

Student comments regarding the READ 180 program:

"When I first started READ 180, I could read, but I didn't understand anything. I could not answer a single question afterwards. My first book, *All in a Day's Work* (28 pages), took me forever to complete. As I went on, I got better, and it seemed easier. I have read 14 books now. One of them was *Hiroshima*, a much more advanced book with 56 pages. After reading it, I saw a documentary about it on TV. Before, I would have bypassed the documentary, but now I wanted to know everything about the topic. READ 180 has opened up a whole new world to me—one I was not interested in knowing about before." —*Robert, a READ 180 student*

"I had no interest in reading at all, and now I just love it. I can't understand my change of attitude. If you had told me months ago that I would be reading for pleasure, I would have told you, you were nuts— basically that you were way out of touch with reality." —*Jack, a READ 180 student*

"This is a great project. I want to do this exclusively." —*Leo, a READ 180 student*

CHAPTER 15

Warden Hosts Westmorland Literacy Project

In the spring of 2003 our warden, Mike Corbett, was so pleased with our progress with the Westmorland Literacy Project that he held a reception at the Beausejour Hotel in Moncton, New Brunswick, to greet the teachers who were using our book packages. This was a huge event for us, as the Beausejour is the classiest hotel in the Moncton area.

The warden opened the festivities by welcoming everyone and acknowledging how much everyone's partnerships meant to us. A representative from Scholastic Books, NYC, Mr. Patrick Daly, was in attendance—sent by Mr. Dick Robinson—and spoke about how pleased the company was to be part of our project. Mr. Daly also spoke about the READ 180 program, the program that he had created and then led the team who implemented it. Mr. Jean-Guy Bourque, regional manager of correctional programs at CSC's regional headquarters, spoke about how the project addressed many of the core values in the CSC mission statement.

Then, Rick and I presented our "best practices" strategies and a video of our work thus far. A couple of inmates—one was a reading tutor, and the other was a reader—spoke about how much they enjoyed the project and how much they liked helping other readers. The inmates also talked about how much hard work it was at the beginning and how it became easier and easier as they got more practice. Without intending to do so, they supported our original hypothesis.

Our warden again addressed the assembly and talked about how the project was a win-win for us and for the community.

"When inmates start giving back to the community, their potential for success in the community increases. While preparation can happen at the institution, reintegration happens in the community. Crime is a community problem. Reintegration is a community solution," he announced.

It was amazing to watch how empowered these men became just by improving their reading skills. Gradually, small changes in attitudes and values started to take place. Men who wanted to be seen as tough and uncaring were suddenly wanting to do well and wanting to give back, as the warden said. It suddenly became important to give back to children, and this project made it possible for the inmates to do that. Many of them stated that, as children, they had never been read to. They thought it would have been nice to experience that as a child, so they wanted to ensure that, with their help, these children would be read to.

We all try just a little harder when we know we are able to help a child.

At the end of the day, the teachers were pleased to have been invited to such a nice event, and their dedication to our project was renewed. We continued to receive good feedback from the teachers.

When the inmate turnaround coordinator received the books back from the public schools, his first task was to inventory all of our materials and make sure that they were all returned in good condition. We were pleased that, for the most part, the children seemed to respect the materials and did not write in the books or deface them in any way. An unexpected bonus was that the children started writing thank-you notes and sending pictures of their interpretations of the books they had listened to. The inmates looked forward to seeing this each month. I still have a binder full of the children's entries.

In the younger grades, the children would send a drawing and a note—written as best as they could—that sometimes named the inmate who had read the book. The children learned the inmates' names because at the start of each tape, the reader would say: "Hello, my name is _____ (first name only) and I am going to read the book _____ by _____."

If a child's note was totally illegible due to their age and inexperience with writing, the teacher would write down a translation of what the child intended to say. Early on in the school year, it was almost impossible to guess what the child wanted to say. As the year went on, the inmates became quite successful in understanding what the child was saying, so they would cover up the teacher's writing while reading the child's note. I think this was a combination of the children getting better at writing and the inmates becoming more familiar with each child's writing. In any case, there was measurable progress on both sides.

When the packages returned, the turnaround coordinator would be swamped by our inmate readers clambering to see if a child had done a drawing from the books they recorded. I would always tell our readers to leave the coordinator alone until he had a chance to inventory everything and send out the next books. The readers had lots of time between the turnarounds to look at the work the children had sent. We always tried to have our new batch of books sent out within a two-day period. The coordinator had to work quickly and diligently for those two days, but after that he had lots of time to either help the reading coach get readers ready to record or view and catalog the children's work. Our readers were welcome to look through the binder of the children's work at any time. Although I have expressed our gratitude to the teachers and their students, I don't think they will ever really understand how much this meant to our inmates.

Once in a while, a teacher would write a note about the program, which we also put into the binder. All of their comments were positive and very much appreciated. The teachers knew that inmates were the readers and that all the materials came from Westmorland Institution on a lending basis. Even teachers who joined the lending service after our initial invitation—where they met us and chose their first books—knew the facts about the program.

It was at the teachers' discretion whether or not to tell the students that this project was performed by inmates. Most of the kindergarten and Grade 1 teachers simply said that some gentlemen, who wanted to help children learn to read, had recorded themselves reading books onto tapes for the schools to use. Some of the teachers, who taught Grade 2 and up, told their students that men in prison made the tapes as part of a prison project to help children learn to read.

One late afternoon, a Grade 3 teacher phoned me to say that she had played one of our tapes in the reading circle and the whole class had listened to the tape together. She said all of a sudden, a little girl jumped up in excitement.

"Miss, that's my dad who is reading. Doesn't he sound great?" the girl exclaimed.

The teacher said she was unsure of what to say because she had told her students that the men reading were inmates. But she said she took her cue from the girl and the other students. They were congratulating the girl and saying her dad was, indeed, doing a great job. The teacher did not identify the girl to me, and I didn't ask. I brought all of my readers together to tell them that someone's third-grade daughter was very proud of her dad. I told them they didn't need to identify who it was because I wasn't even sure if the reader was still with us or had been paroled. No one took credit for it, so I suspect that he had been released. One thing that means a lot to any inmate is his family. If he had still been with us, I have no doubt he would have come forward and said how much it meant to him that his daughter was proud of him.

I documented this as I realized this was another inroad into good feeling about the project within the community.

At the two-year mark for our project, Rick said to me, "Rosemary, you have to have a name."

We had been calling the work we were doing, the Westmorland Literacy Project.

"This is not a project anymore. It is now a program. You must name it," Rick said.

"What? I get to name it?" I asked.

"Of course, you get to name it. It is your project," Rick said.

When the warden hosted the welcoming party at the Beausejour, we had been interviewed by reporters and one of them wrote the headline: "Inmates at Westmorland Turning a New Page." I thought that this was really powerful—these words signified a new beginning, as well as the literal context of turning book pages while listening to the cassette tapes.

I told Rick that my program's name would be: Turning a New Page. He liked my choice so much that he legally put his whole consulting business under that title. And it is, to this day, the name of his company.

CHAPTER 16

Piloting Cracking the Code

Before working at Westmorland Institution, I owned a tutoring business where I worked with a lot of French immersion students. In French, there are only 26 phonemes (different sounds), and all words are made up of different letter combinations that make these sounds. I explained to Rick that when teaching children to read in French, I would instruct them to put together letter combinations that made a single sound in order to decode the word and pronounce it correctly.

For example, the word "beau" would look like this: b̲e̲a̲u̲, where the "b" would make the single "b" sound and the *eau* would make the single long *o* sound. Therefore, the word would be pronounced as "bo" with a long *o*—it has four letters but only two sounds.

After hearing this, Rick who is a reading specialist and consultant in English, said that he would start researching similar patterns in English. We worked together on this and developed a program, which he named Cracking the Code. He asked if I would pilot this program in my classroom at Westmorland Institution. I was eager to administer it. And I thought it could only augment everything that I was already working towards, as I did have students with some reading and learning problems in spite of being at the grade 7 and 8 level.

Cracking the Code is a visual marking system based on letter patterns. It requires recognizing and marking patterns while stating aloud what is being marked and why. There are 12 patterns that are marked from 12 to one or the last pattern learned to the first pattern learned. The learner does not attempt to pronounce or read any of the words until completing the "r" pattern, which is the seventh pattern. Students must mark the words according to the taught patterns while reciting what they are doing with each mark. The statement itself is patterned, and the students should not deviate from the pattern.

For example, take the word *bend*. The learner would say: "I am marking the *e* as short because a vowel by itself is usually short. I am underlining nd as one, consonants that go together, and I am underlining the b because it is a consonant. This is what it looks like now: b ĕ nd.

The patterns are taught one at a time. When marking a word, students work backwards from the last pattern taught through to the first pattern. With the marking and the repetition, students begin to gain confidence because they are able to do exactly what is expected of them. There is no confusion, and there are no exceptions. The students do not second guess asking themselves if they need to mark a certain letter or if this is a case where the letter is an exception.

In our observations of struggling readers, we noted that readers never knew if what they were trying to read or decode was a rule or an exception to that rule. But with Cracking the Code there are no rules to learn and therefore no exceptions. Without needing to question this, the readers' uncertainty transforms into confidence in their own abilities. This program takes the guesswork out of the equation. The other advantage to this program is that it is visual, and students never have to try to say the word until they pass the "r" patterns at number seven. By that time, needing to say the word out loud is no longer a problem, and the learner is no longer threatened by the fear of saying it incorrectly. It is so neat to witness the "no longer struggling" readers become empowered and proud of their accomplishments.

This is an example of Cracking the Code. This is pattern number 3, and this is what the students see on page 9 of their workbooks.

One Vowel

New Pattern: A vowel by itself is usually short.
Use ˘ to mark the vowel. Example: hŭg

2. Underline, as one, consonants that go together.
3. Underline the consonants.

1. hot   jump   shop   best   get

2. mist   rat   lamp   dusk   tub

There are three more lines of words that the students must mark while stating what they are doing for each mark.

Examples:

1. hot The student would say, "I am using a short˘ over the o because a vowel by itself is usually short. There are no consonants that go together. I am underlining h and t because they are consonants." The word now looks like this: h̆ŏt.

   2. mist The student would say, "I am using a short˘ over the i because a vowel by itself is usually short. I am underlining st, consonants that go together. I am underlining m because it is a consonant." The word now looks like this: mĭst.

Note: In example number 1, there were no consonants that go together; therefore, the students would say, "There are no consonants that go together …" In the repetition of saying what they are doing, the students do not skip any steps. If there are no letters representing a pattern in the progression of working from the last pattern to the first, the students must note that as part of the pattern of what they are doing.

When I piloted Cracking the Code in my classroom at Westmorland Institution, I talked to my class ahead of time. I told them that we had been asked to pilot a reading program where we were to find any mistakes, as well as identify any weaknesses in the program. It meant that we got to test out the new materials and act as the quality-control people ensuring that the program was sound. This appealed to my students, and I must say they were vigilant in finding even minor errors.

   At the time, I had a student, Fred, who had completed Grade 7 and Grade 8 math, Grade 8 science, and Grade 7, and Grade 8 reading and

English grammar skills. All he had left to complete in level two were the grades 7 and 8 writing components. But he refused. He would not write. No amount of encouragement from me could entice him to tackle the writing portion.

One morning, I asked him why he would not even try. He said he could not write because he could not spell. I told him that he was a good storyteller so he should just write the way he would talk. Again, he said he would not because he could not spell. Even when I told him to just write it the way he thought it should be spelled since we could edit it afterwards, he would not try.

Three and a half weeks into Cracking the Code, Fred was about to leave class for the day when he openly stated that he loved the program. A week after that, I handed him the whiteboard marker and asked him to write the word "incarceration" on the board. Keep in mind, Fred had always had trouble spelling three- or four-letter words, and now I was asking him to spell a 13-letter word on the board in front of the whole class. I could tell my other students were angry, thinking that I was setting him up—something I would never do.

"Fred, you don't have to do it," one student said.

Fred walked confidently to me, took the marker, stood in front of the board, and wrote: "incarseration."

"Is it correct?" he asked, turning to me.

"It is phonetically correct, but one letter is wrong," I said.

He turned back to the board and erased the "s" to replace it with a "c." Now the word on the board read: "incarceration." Fred did not ask again if it was correct because he knew that it was. I must mention that when he wrote the word on the board, there was no hesitation. He wrote it as fast as he could put the letters there.

That evening, I phoned Rick to tell him about this and how I had found this program to be an excellent spelling tool. He told me not to promote Cracking the Code as a spelling tool—it was a reading tool. I told him that in piloting Cracking the Code, I had found it to be an excellent tool for both reading and spelling and would continue to use it for both in my work at Westmorland Institution.

Outside of the classroom, being able to write meant a lot for Fred. One morning, he came to class and told me that his mom had called him to ask why he finally dictated a letter for another inmate to write for him to send to her after 21 years of incarceration. (Fred was a lifer.) He told her he did not dictate it—he had written it himself. He told her that since he was following a new program at school, he could now spell. Therefore, he could now write. He told me that his Mom cried. I thought that was a powerful story. Fred was so thankful for being included in the program that he promoted it to other learners who had difficulty. Students were approaching me to get involved. Through the work shift board, I hired a tutor to follow the program with us in class (for one half-hour session a day), and at the end of it, I turned the program over to him to teach. He really believed in the program and did an excellent job working with students both in small groups and one-to-one.

Here is another story about Cracking the Code.

One Monday morning, I welcomed four new students in my class. One of Mary King's newcomers, Lee, who was to be in the literacy class, approached me and said his teacher had told him to talk to me. I told him that he should wait in his assigned classroom until I settled my own newcomers, and then I would find him.

Forty-five minutes later, I led him to my office and asked what I could do for him.

"I can't come to school," Lee said.

I asked him why not. He sat forward in his chair and put his face in his hands. I was really busy that morning, and I was needed elsewhere in the school, but I sensed that I needed to hear what this man had to say. I sat, and I waited and waited some more.

Just when I thought he was going to stay that way all morning, he looked up at me and took a big breath.

"Okay, I'm going to tell you why I can't come to school. I can't read. I wish I could, but I have tried and tried, and I can't be taught. Everyone in my life, including my wife, has tried to teach me. I have failed every time. I am almost 37 years old and I have accepted it. But every new person I meet thinks they can help me. I am tired of failing just to prove to people that I can't do it," Lee said.

"Okay, will you agree to stay in school for two weeks? I will get you to work with a tutor on a program that my brother and I created. At the end of two weeks if you haven't seen any progress, I will personally write a work shift for you and clear it with your parole officer so that you may leave school. At the end of two weeks, you will not be able to read, but you should see some progress," I said.

"I will stay for the two weeks and not one second longer," he said.

I told him we had a deal.

I sent him back to his classroom while I arranged for the tutor. I chose Liam as Lee's tutor, and they got along great right from the start.

On the second day, Lee told Liam, "I need to work with you on this f—king bullshit for two weeks, and then I can get out of school. I made a deal with the teacher in charge."

Liam told me this after their session. To his credit, Lee worked hard and attended his half-day morning sessions on time. On June 20—the last day of the two weeks—Lee's literacy teacher, Mary King, came to my office.

"Rosemary, Lee just asked me for a work shift," Mary said.

My heart sank. "Mary, he doesn't see any progress at all in two weeks?" I asked.

A big smile crossed Mary's face. "Rosemary, he wants a work shift to come to school full time. He said that this program works and he needed every second he could get of it before he got paroled."

Mary and I did a happy high-five dance in my office as we were both overjoyed. Then, Mary continued to tell me about her conversation with Lee.

"And you know that other teacher? She was not right. She said I wouldn't be reading at the end of the two weeks. I can read all of the beginner reader books in the Turning a New Page room. I can read word lists to my wife on the phone. I can read!" Lee said to Mary.

I told Mary that this was one time where it was my pleasure to be wrong! Then, we both got back to work.

On the following Monday, Liam came to see me in my office and said that on Friday he asked Lee how this *f—king bullshit* was working for him now. Liam told me that Lee said,

"This f—king bullshit is boss, man!"

I had to write this in Lee's own words because anyone who has worked with inmates understands the honesty and the power behind those words. Yet another case where Cracking the Code saved the day!

CHAPTER 17

The Portfolio Development Program

In September 2005, Westmorland Institution was offered the Portfolio Development Program through the Prior Learning Assessment (PLA) Centre in Halifax, Nova Scotia. Dan Smyth, assistant warden of correctional programs, whom I have mentioned many times before, asked Mary King, the literacy teacher, and me to oversee the program. In order to do so, Mary and I had to take the course as students, by actively participating in completing the assignments and contributing during class. We took the class with eight inmates, and we shared our experiences and resumes under the direction of Katherine, teacher representative for the PLA Centre.

It was a 10-week course, occurring one afternoon per week in the literacy class. So, the literacy class and the level two class would shut down for the afternoon. Mary and I enjoyed the class very much, but we were glad that it was only once a week because the workload for it was very heavy and time-consuming. At the end of the 10 weeks, we received two certificates: one for the course itself, and the other certifying that we were trained for delivery.

On the second last week of the program, we were all required to hand in our portfolio binders for assessment. Katherine critiqued mine saying that I needed a title page to identify whose binder it was. I showed her my name on the spine of the binder. She said that was fine, but when she opened the book, she wanted to see the first page indicating who I was— not just my name. She told me to be creative and have the page ready when she returned next week for the last class.

Being a bit miffed and somewhat sarcastic, I made a title page that looked like this:

Rosemary Alice McAtee Pineau

(daughter, sister, wife, mother, aunt, sister-in-law, daughter-in-law, grandmother, teacher, administrator)

I thought Katherine would mildly rebuke me for being way over the top. That was not the case. Katherine offered high praise for my title page and said it was just what she was looking for. She said that she felt that she knew quite a bit about me from that one page.

When I told her that I was being petty and sarcastic, we both laughed.

"Well, that worked!" Katherine said.

Mary and I taught the Portfolio Program several times after that. We tried to run it twice a year: once in the spring and once in the fall. It was a wonderful program, and it was a great way for inmates to recognize and channel the positive things they had done in their lives. Before the end of the program, we taught them how to create a skills-based resume, rather than a chronological-based one. A chronological resume citing the years that education or work occurred, emphasizes gaps in the years that would need to be explained as times of incarceration. A skills-based resume focuses on what they are able to do and what they can offer the employer.

This is an example of a skills-based resume. Titles are highlighted and then relevant qualifications are listed. Dates are not used in a skills-based resume.

Rosemary Pineau

Career Objective: Instructor or Training Officer for Adults

Highlights of Qualifications:

- 25 years teaching in a federal prison
- 44 years teaching experience (all levels)

- Strong communication skills
- Exceptional organizational skills
- Enthusiastic educator

This is how to start a skills-based resume. Several more highlights would be used with each of their qualifications listed. This gives employers the information they need in an easy-to-read presentation. It also allows inmates to highlight their strengths without needing to account for missing dates (times of incarceration).

Legally, in Canada, if an employer asks if you have been incarcerated, you must respond truthfully. But if not asked, you are not required to volunteer that information. Often if the parolee is given a chance, he is able to do well. Once the employer has seen his skills, it is easier and safer to divulge past incarceration(s). Hopefully, by that time, the employer recognizes the employee as a valued, trusted, and dependable part of the team.

In teaching this Portfolio Program, often students would say, "I can't make a resume. I don't have any skills."

"You're 35 years old. If you had no skills, you would not be alive," I would respond.

Once Mary and I suggested skills and helped inmates create professional-looking resumes, they would be so proud of this document that they would just beam.

It was a program that required a lot of work and a great deal of introspection, but in the end, it was very beneficial for the inmates who participated. When they completed the program, they left with a professional resume, their portfolio binder, and all of their assignments and documents on a disc for further use in the community. I saw this as a great service for them, and it turned out that it was a service that was greatly appreciated. We heard back from several men who told us that because of that program, they got jobs to support themselves and their families.

Leaving prison and not being able to gain employment right away presents lots of problems. Often, the stress leads the parolee back to reoffending as it's the easiest route to make money. So, being able to walk into a job straight out of prison is a big deal. Those who are fortunate enough to do that have a better chance of assimilating back into the community, and they are further along on the road to becoming successful, participating members of their neighborhood, town, province, and country.

CHAPTER 18

Literacy Days

Every September, Literacy Day is celebrated internationally. At Westmorland Institution, we initiated different literacy challenges to keep students interested and to ensure their participation. On August 11, 2004, I issued a challenge for readers to read one million words by September 8: Literacy Day. Any inmate at the institution could participate—he did not have to be a student in the school.

For my challenge, I asked one of my reading coaches, Tony, if he would be the coordinator, to record the number of words read. Tony would enroll the reader and allow him to sign out books. Then, he would check the word count. Some of the books displayed the word count at the front of the book, but if the book did not provide the word count, Tony would count the words on one page and multiply by the number of pages.

I allotted one month for this project because I didn't know how many inmates would want to participate. If I only had a couple of participants, I had to allow enough time for them to accomplish the task—I never set anyone up to fail. This project, however, caught on immediately. At all times of the day, inmates were coming over to the school to find Tony to sign up and borrow books. It was surprising, but great to see. Students in class would get their work done and pull out their private reading books.

"Nobody does anything else at night in our units, but read. No TV, no cards, no chatting. Just reading," one student told me.

Tony told me that some guys were chasing him down in the evenings to give him their word counts. But Tony would tell them to inform him about the word count at school from 8 a.m. to11:30 a.m. or 1 p.m. to 4:00 p.m.

He said he would be bench pressing in the gym, and he would hear some excited voice calling, "Tony, Tony, I read 650 words!"

Tony found it to be frustrating and sometimes rather annoying, but he was a good sport and the best coordinator I could have picked for that type of a project. I was pleased that the project had taken off so well. From early on, I always said that when working with inmates if I asked for something, they always gave way more than I asked for.

By Literacy Day, our word count was over 14 million—14 times more than what I had asked for.

We had a great Literacy Day celebration. The warden opened the festivities by welcoming our guests and congratulating our participants on the reading challenge. Our guests included Nina Gamble (administrative assistant for Excalibur Learning Resource Center, which was the company that employed us—Westmorland Institution teachers), Rick McAtee (my brother and owner of Turning a New Page), and Karen Forsythe (a representative from Scholastic Books). Karen read the Scholastic children's book *How Much Is a Million?* written by David M. Schwartz and illustrated by Steven Kellogg. All of the reading participants had signed the book, and Karen presented it to the warden after reading it to the audience.

Rick joined me in a meeting with Dan Smyth, the assistant warden of programs, and we agreed that Westmorland Institution would celebrate Literacy Day on the second Friday in September. In so doing, we would not be competing for Literacy Day with public schools celebrating it the first week of September. That way, public-school representatives could possibly attend our event.

Over the years, we always thought of a way to celebrate. In 2006, I issued a challenge to write a limerick, which was one of the poetry-writing styles we touched on in the level two English program. This was a bit challenging for some, and we didn't get as many participants as we had had for other literacy days. We got enough participation, though, for the event.

To tackle this challenge, participants needed to understand the basic concept of limericks. They needed to know that a limerick consisted of five lines—the first, second and fifth lines rhyme with each other, while the second-and-third lines rhyme with each other but not with the other three lines.

Here is a sample of some of our entries:

Here in the school at Westmorlin'
Education is what teachers' concernin.'
I would come every day
During my stay
To do all my time by learnin.'

There once was a pauper named Meg
Who accidentally lost her leg.
Her friends said they should
Make her a leg of wood
After which they would call her "Peg."

There once was a teacher named Mary,
Who said: "On your way to school, don't tarry.
For if you are late,
Over the intercom, you, I will berate
And your pay will drop something scary."

Once upon a time in a faraway land,
Adventures untwirled with a wave of his hand.
The beasts came alive,
Where the strong survive
And now reading has a new number one fan.

When our Literacy Day activities were open to the public, my Mom, Kay McAtee, would come from Maine to attend. She has always had a keen interest in literacy and she volunteered at several of the elementary schools in Millinocket, Maine, to read to the children.

The first time she came to the institution, I took her on a tour of the school, showing her various academic and program classrooms and offices. Walking through the hall, she looked at the facilities with interest.

"This looks just like a school!" she exclaimed with surprise.

"Mom, this is a school." I said.

As the day went on, Mom interacted with quite a few of our students (inmates). They were all very respectful, almost in awe that she was my mom.

It has been my experience in working with inmates, that when people come in from the general public, all of the inmates are on their best behavior. They figuratively "roll out the red carpet." They want "guest(s)" to feel comfortable and maybe to forget that they are speaking with inmates. The inmates want to garner respect and acceptance.

At the end of the day, Mom was extremely impressed with the whole situation, from the facilities, to the other staff, to the inmates.

"If people could see how much these men have to offer and how hard they are working to improve, they would be greatly impressed," she said.

I was happy that she had enjoyed the day. After that, whenever we had an open-to-the-public school celebration, Mom attended.

In 2007, for Literacy Day, we wrote and illustrated children's books. I hired a tutor, Paul, to help the writers get their thoughts on paper and then format it on the computer with the illustrations. I told Paul that he should write some books himself so that he could better help the students with their ideas and plot lines. He was very good at helping out, but when it came to trying it himself, he was lost. He kept asking what he should write about. I would offer him some suggestions, and he would walk away, only to return saying he had no inspiration.

One day, he approached me at a moment when I was really busy and had no patience for him or anyone else interrupting my thought process.

"I can't come up with anything. What can I write about?" he asked.

"I don't know, Paul. I have given you all kinds of suggestions and you keep coming back with nothing. Go away and write about the Easter Bunny who wanted to be Santa Claus," I answered in frustration.

He looked at me for a few moments. "I can do that!" he said.

Paul wrote a wonderful children's tale with that title. After completing his first book, he took off with ideas and stories that could delight any child. Paul wrote 14 books. Then, for some infraction, he had been taken to higher security, just next door at Dorchester Medium-Security Penitentiary. But due to his dedicated participation to this project, I requested that he be able to attend the Literacy Day festivities where we showcased 40 children's books that were written and illustrated by inmates. Fourteen of those books were written and illustrated by Paul, and he had a hand in quite a few of the other books through his tutoring and assistance. At my request, he was escorted to Westmorland Institution for the celebration.

"This is the best project we have ever done. Guys actually care if they should use a period or a comma and are willing to research or ask," said Mary King, the literacy teacher.

On Literacy Day in 2008, we honored Senator Marilyn Trenholme Counsell, who was retiring. She had attended several of our literacy celebrations and had been a strong advocate for literacy during her working capacity as New Brunswick's lieutenant governor, which she carried over to her duties as senator. She had always encouraged our inmates and made them feel capable of giving back. Literacy was very close to her heart, and she told the audience that literacy was one of the most powerful things.

Her direct quote was, "Reading is the way to contentment and empowerment."

Senator Marilyn read us a book entitled *The Cremation of Sam McGee* by Robert Service, and then gave the book as a gift to us for our school. She was pleased and surprised when both inmates and staff presented her with a basket full of "memories" to take forward into her retirement. She was a great support to us for years, and it was fun for us to show our appreciation.

Every Literacy Day, we planned a special way to celebrate. Sometimes it was just an in-house event for the school. Other times, it was open for guests as noted above. But we always honored the day.

CHAPTER 19

Cloth Envelopes

For Turning a New Page, when sending out our books and tapes to the schools, we put four books with one cassette tape into each package. The package was a plastic envelope with a string tie around a button—the envelope also had a small window where we could place an index card with the title of the book. This worked well for quite a while.

But as we sent out packages more and more frequently, the envelopes started to easily rip. As this occurred several years into our lending process, the envelopes were becoming brittle and ripping easily due to age, not due to vandalism by the children. I told the turnaround coordinator not to send out ripped envelopes since I had a good supply of new envelopes to replace the worn ones. He later said to me that we were running out of new ones and more envelopes were coming back damaged.

I gathered the Turning a New Page crew together to brainstorm ideas to solve this problem. One of my inmate employees suggested cloth bags, so we explored this possibility. Dan Smyth, assistant warden of correctional programs, told me to go to Supply and Services (SIS), and they would make the bags for us. He told me to create a prototype to show the work supervisor who would supervise inmates in the making of new bags for us in his shop.

After creating the prototype, I brought the supplies to the SIS supervisor, who was in charge of managing the inmates working in the SIS shop. He told me his inmate staff couldn't work on the cloth bags because he needed them to work on other tasks. He asked how many bags we would need— when I told him a minimum of 200, he just laughed. I informed Dan, who suggested that I ask the supervisor if my inmate employees could use his sewing machines to make the cloth bags. He graciously allowed us to use his machines when his staff was working on something else.

Okay, we could do this job!

On a Tuesday morning, I sent two of my employees, Joe and Keith, to SIS with the template and materials they needed. Joe and Keith were excited to work on this job. They were gone for most of the morning, and I was dying to know how they were doing.

When they returned to school, they were both downhearted. They had tried, unsuccessfully, all morning to sew one envelope. The SIS machines were too strong and kept sucking the fabric down into the feed dogs. They had tried different thread tensions, but it was of no use—the machines were for industrial strength fabric. We needed an ordinary household sewing machine.

Again, I informed Dan, and he sent me next door to Dorchester Medium Security Penitentiary to implore their SIS supervisor to use his machines. Dan had called ahead of time, and the SIS supervisor was expecting me. Alas, it was the same thing there. They only had heavy-duty industrial machines as well. Why would we have thought differently?

After all of this, I called around the area looking to rent a sewing machine. It was very cost prohibitive. I have sewn since I was a young child and used my mom's sewing machine while living at home. When I went to university, my parents bought me a portable machine. In 1980, when I was a mom of two and expecting a third, I bought a new machine—the one I have to this day. It is an Omega sewing machine and at that time, it cost almost $700—an exorbitant price, but well worth the cost considering how much I used it and still do. But discovering that rental prices were so high, one of the potential leasers advised me to just buy a sewing machine. I took this suggestion and went to Walmart expecting the price to be over a $1,000. To my great surprise, I could buy an Omega (same brand as mine at home) for less than $200. When have you heard of the price of an item, like that, going down?

Dan was always in the loop when we wanted to do new things in the school. If we did not have his approval, we did not proceed. He was very supportive and almost always gave approval for new innovation in creating fun and interesting ways for the inmates to learn and/or work. In the chain of command, the AWCP was the person I was required to consult on anything new. Dan held that position for many of the years that I taught at Westmorland Institution.

I informed Dan of the cost of the sewing machine, and he gave me petty cash to buy it. So, I hired two inmates, through the work shift board, one to cut fabric and one to sew. We were in business. Production took place in the Turning a New Page room during the summer while public schools were out for summer vacation. Now, our goal was to have enough bags ready for the September turnaround. The employees worked all summer, and by fall we made enough bags to start off the school year.

The bags which looked similar to long Manila envelopes, were rectangular with a V-shaped closure that was fastened with a small piece of Velcro in the front. On the front left side about one-third of the way down, we sewed a plastic window the size of an index card. The right side of the window remained open so we could insert the index card with the book title. Thus, we were able to switch out the index cards if we needed to do so. We used a cardboard template to cut the pieces to the specifications. There was some trial and error to get the correct needle and tension on the thread to sew on the plastic windows, but my employees were not ones to give up until the problem was solved. And solve it, they did!

When school started up and we sent out our book packages, I sent a memo to the teachers to note our new envelope presentation.

After the first turnaround, I got a call from Katherine Jacks, the Anglophone East School District First Steps trainer (District 2 School Board, and the early years supervisor title had both been renamed). This was some time around 2005 or 2006.

"Rosemary, where did you get your cloth envelopes?" she asked.

"I had them made," I said.

"Where?" she asked.

"Right here at the institution."

"You have staff there making cloth envelopes for you?" She asked with surprise.

"No, I have inmate workers making them."

There was a long pause. "Are they men?" she asked.

"This is a male prison. All of the inmates are men," I said.

After an even longer pause, she asked, "Do you think they could do a sewing project for us?"

I asked her to send me a prototype of what she wanted and I would get back to her. At noon the next day, I had the prototype—an over-the-chair bag to hang off the back of students' chairs with pockets to store small items, such as pencils, erasers, etc.—sitting on my desk along with two samples of fabric. I gave these items to my employees.

The next day, the school district trainer had the finished product back on her desk by noon. She phoned me right away.

"The two samples that your inmates made are better than the prototype. What do we need to do for them to take on this project for us?" she asked.

I asked her how many chair bags she would need. She said she would find out from the teachers, but it could amount to quite a few. Each teacher would want a class set of between 25 to 30. I told her that she would have to provide the fabric and the thread. We would provide the labor. This was a great new adventure for us and yet another link to the community—one more way our inmates were able to give back.

This project took off in a great way!

The school district trainer would select and pay for fabric and thread from Fabricville, a Moncton fabric store, and then she would phone me when the items were ready to be picked up. I would arrange for our institutional drivers to pick up the order, and they would arrive at the school carrying several five-foot-long bolts of fabric, asking where we wanted it.

It was so much fun. Once we got underway, it grew into such a big project that I had to ask for another sewing machine. Again, this was approved by Dan and paid for by the institution. After receiving the extra sewing machine, I then asked the work shift board for another sewer. I had one cutter and two sewers working in the Turning a New Page room. One of my sewers, Doug, was very eager. He was a dedicated worker and set goals for himself. One of his goals was to make 25 bags a day. I told him that he didn't need to work fast, but rather he needed to make the bags perfectly. He assured me that the bags would be perfect while reaching his daily personal goal of 25.

One day, I went into the Turning a New Page room and saw him scoring a fold.

"Show me your thumb," I said to Doug.

He held it up. "Doesn't that hurt?" I asked.

He said that it did hurt when he first started but it was okay now. This was a revelation to me, and I wondered why I had not taken this into account before. I had been sewing since I was eight years old, and I never went near the sewing machine without first setting up the ironing board and plugging in the iron. I asked myself what I was thinking by not providing this for my workers.

The next day, I brought in a tabletop ironing board and an iron. I then hired a presser, through the work shift board. This allowed Doug to up his personal goal to 30 bags a day. The school district, including the teachers and the students, were all happy with our work, so we kept receiving more and more fabric. We loved doing this, and we were never overwhelmed by it. By the end of the project, we had made more than 4,000 bags.

The day before Doug was paroled, he came to the school to talk to me. He told me how much his job at Turning a New Page had meant to him. Being able to get up in the morning and go to work in a respected position where you knew that your job mattered—not only to your immediate supervisor, but also to children, parents, teachers, and the community at large—gave him a sense of pride, purpose, and satisfaction. He said he started developing self-worth again and believing that he did, in fact, have something to contribute.

Doug was a great employee. He sewed more than half of the 1,600 over-the-chair bags that we had made up to that point. And he also worked with two groups of students on Cracking the Code. He was always pleasant and cooperative. He always had a good idea, and he never let me down or missed deadlines. When he left, I missed his sense of humor and optimism, as well as his dedication. I hope he is successful and happy.

CHAPTER 20

The Writing Steps to Success

When students wrote their GED tests, there were two subject areas they found difficult—the writing skills test and to a lesser extent, the math test. The writing skills test was composed of two parts: 60 multiple-choice questions and a 200-word essay on a given topic. Students were given two hours to complete the two portions. Most of the students who did not pass believed that it was due to the essay portion of the test. Although the mark was not broken down according to the two separate parts, the student needed to pass both portions of the test to achieve a passing mark.

When Rick notified me that he had been working on a writing skills book that he wanted me to pilot at Westmorland Institution, I was happy to help. Right away, Rick sent me all the materials to pilot the project. Reader, you may be noticing a pattern here—Rick and I would often share resources because his work with children and teachers and my work with inmates created a win-win situation for both of us. We were happy to pilot programs and be the guinea pigs working out the kinks, while reaping the benefits of new innovative resources. I could always persuade the inmates to buy into piloting a project because it made them feel respected and important, especially when they could find a small error or a typo.

Rick's program is called The Writing Steps to Success. It includes a teacher's manual and student workbooks. In a very easy way, the mechanics of writing are taught by starting with a list of words and ending with concluding sentences five steps later. It teaches the learner that an organized, efficient way to write does not have to be fraught with fear and apprehension.

This is the progression of steps followed in the guideline for The Writing Steps to Success:

- Step 1 - Words
- Step 2 - Phrases
- Step 3 - Sentences
- Step 4 - Supporting Sentences
- Step 5 - Concluding Sentences

The teacher's guide to teaching all of the steps in a patterned manner is concise and thorough; the student's workbook is well-laid-out and easy to follow.

When I piloted this program at Westmorland Institution, I did it a bit differently from other pilots I had administered. I did not make this program compulsory but rather left it open for students who wanted to take part. I had a limit of 10 students. Every afternoon, I taught the program from 1:30 p.m. to 2:00 p.m. in a classroom within the program area, which was down the hall from my own classroom. This meant that I assigned work to my unsupervised class for a half hour each afternoon. Mary King, the literacy teacher, whose classroom was right next door to mine, agreed to periodically look in on my class. My students were respectful as they acted appropriately and did not cause any problems while I was working with the pilot group.

In the pilot class, I had four GED students, four level two (my class) students, and two literacy students. All four of the GED students had written the GED tests but had not passed the writing skills test, which was the only test that kept them from obtaining their GED certificate.

On the third day, two of the GED students dropped out. They said the program was too elementary and they were far above this level. I let them go without trying to encourage them to stay. My half hour away from my own class could not be spent in cajoling students to see the merits of the program. The students needed to buy into the program and put forth their best efforts. The other eight students did just that and saw the program to the end. All eight students were grateful to have followed the program and believed they had made progress.

When the next GED tests were written at the institution, the two students who completed Writing Steps to Success passed their writing skills test. And they received their GED certificates. They were thrilled and made sure to thank me for the program and the help. The two students who quit still did not pass and did not receive their GED certificates. So, they both approached me and asked to be included in the next class that I would teach. I told them that I needed to limit the class to 10 people—and I would include them only if I had room. I was not willing to bump someone else because I could not trust that these two students would complete the program.

As it happened, I had room for the two students. They completed the program, rewrote the GED tests, and successfully achieved their GED certificates. Both were grateful.

Word had gone around Westmorland Institution that I was teaching a really neat writing course, and other inmates—some who were not even in school—had signed up. After getting permission from Dan, I told them they were welcome to join if they could be away from their jobs for half an hour each day. It was their responsibility to clear it with their work supervisors. I received calls from some of the supervisors to verify that this was real. With my assurance, the supervisors graciously allowed their workers to take part. Parole officers were advised that inmates on their caseloads were following the program and credit was given by way of reports in Offender Management System (OMS) and a completion certificate from the program.

I taught the course several times after the initial pilot, and everyone who took it was pleased with their results. One participant said that he thought writing was such a hardship, but then he discovered that it was fun. Another said that he never knew one could be taught to write—he thought you could either write or you couldn't, and he believed he was one who couldn't.

Here is another story about The Writing Steps to Success—although it is not related to Westmorland Institution, it delves into one of my experiences with the program.

Every January, I visit Rick at his home in Tucson, Arizona, for two weeks. During one of my visits, he had an appointment to present The Writing Steps to Success at an elementary school in Douglas, which is a couple of hours away from Tucson. He invited me to go along. His colleague, Lynnette, also joined us.

On the way there, Rick told me that he would like me to teach one of the sessions. I agreed and did not let on that this would be a problem. He could have taken me to the highest-security prison possible, and I would have felt comfortable meeting, teaching, and working with any inmate there. But grade four children? I was scared. I knew what to expect from inmates—but I did not know what to expect from a class of Grade 4 children. Granted, I already had five children of my own, so I was comfortable with children either one-to-one or in small groups. However, I was not experienced with teaching a whole class of Grade 4 children, and I was not sure what I could expect them to already know or how far I should push them to learn what I would be teaching.

I did not let on to Rick and Lynnette that I was terrified.

When it was time for me to teach my session, I introduced myself to the children, and we got underway. I told them that we would make a list of 20 words related to the weather. Douglas is a town in Arizona where they experience all types of weather from bright sunshine to heavy rains to snow storms and everything in between. So, I didn't think they would have any trouble making the list. I chose students to come forward and write a weather word on the board. It was a long, slow process.

I could not understand why it took so long for Grade 4 children to come up with a word. The chosen student would walk up to the board, excited to be taking part and then stand there, contemplating for the longest time before writing a word on the board. It was taking so long that I thought their time with me would end before we had thought of all the words. Therefore, after every third word, I would write a word on the board myself before calling on the next student. The students were great—they were respectful of each other and of me. And it was a good, fun experience for me. Once we had the 20 words, the rest of the lesson went well, and I left on a good note.

On the way back to Tucson—once the experience was over, and I was still alive—I opened up to Rick and Lynnette that I had had so much apprehension about doing it. Rick said if I had told him I didn't want to teach the session, he wouldn't have been upset. He hadn't realized that I was timid about it. I was glad that they hadn't realized because that meant that I could step outside my comfort zone without appearing foolish!

I did think, though, Rick could have given me a heads-up that the class was composed of 80 percent English Language Learners (ELL) with the majority being Spanish. That explained their hesitation in making up the word list. Rick and Lynnette thought this was a hilarious joke to have played on me, but they both said I did a good job presenting the lesson.

After the fact, I had no choice but to be a good sport about it.

When I returned to work after my vacation in Arizona, I told my class about how I trembled at the thought of teaching children. I told them I was happy to be back with them doing what I knew how to do. Several of my students said they were glad I was back, too. I told them I would take that as a compliment. I did not say that I knew how much inmates dislike any kind of change and how well they relate to their own teacher. But I did note to them that sometimes we all need to go outside of our comfort zones to make progress.

One inmate said he was outside his comfort zone every day just by being in school. And that inmate did put forth the effort and did reap the rewards by completing my class, moving on to the GED class, and acquiring his GED certificate before being released to the community. To think he had started in level one: Grade 4 math. He was a real success story for us, having gone through all three classes with all three of us teachers!

CHAPTER 21

Stories from the Farm

Until 2010, Westmorland Institution had been a working farm, complete with all the usual farm amenities. It had a dairy barn, a beef barn, a piggery, a poultry barn, an abattoir, and crop farming. It also had a greenhouse. All of these locations served as job sites for the inmates.

At Westmorland Institution, the rule was that the inmates had to either work or attend school and programs. They were not allowed to lie around idle during the day. Some inmates attended school on a half-day basis and worked on the farm the other half of the day. Therefore, we got to hear lots of farm stories.

Here are a few stories that I have laughed over more than once.

One afternoon, my classroom tutor came into class and said, "Rosemary, she's right in love with me."

"Who?" I asked.

"Ellie, one of the cows I work with at the dairy barn," Roy said.

"Maybe this story is not appropriate for the classroom," I said.

"It's not like that," he laughed. "Here's what happened. She always follows me around everywhere I go. When I'm mucking out the stalls, she's right there beside me. When I go outside the barn, I look around and again, she is right there beside me. Well, this morning I made the mistake of turning my back on her and all of a sudden—*plop!* A big hoof comes down on my left shoulder. It almost took me to my knees. Before I could react—*plop!* Another big hoof comes down on my right shoulder, and now I am flat on my face down in the dirt. If it wasn't for the two other inmates working there, who helped get her off me, I'd still be down there."

We all laughed at his story.

"The moral is—never turn your back on Ellie," one of the students said. This, of course, brought more laughter.

One day, it was around 12:30 p.m.—still lunchtime—when an inmate came to the school looking for me. He was told that I was in my office and given directions to get there. He knocked on my door, which was slightly ajar. I told him to come in.

He entered and immediately went down on his knees.

"Rosemary, I'm begging you to hire me," he said. "I need a job. I can't go back to the dairy barn. I was assigned there and spent the morning helping the work supervisor who was artificially inseminating cows. He told me, 'Hold this.' And when I looked, it was the tail that he wanted me to hold. I pulled my sleeve down as far as I could over my hand, and the supervisor asked what I was doing. I told him I couldn't touch the tail with my bare hands. He just shook his head. Then he put on a long glove and inserted his hand and arm—almost up to his elbow—inside the cow. I had my face turned away, and the supervisor asked, 'What are you doing now?' I told him I was doing my best not to lose my breakfast.

Please, Rosemary, please hire me. The correctional officer in the Control Center told me to come and see you. He thought you might be willing to hire me. I have a community college diploma in IT, and I will do anything to help out at the school."

I was stunned by this encounter and then so amused by his story, as well as his delivery that I could hardly keep from laughing. I told him he had a great knack for comedy. He asked if that would get him a job with me. We talked at length about requirements and my expectations of my tutors. I told him he would need to be a cut above the average inmate, and I would need to be able to trust him.

I told him I had a reading coach position available. He would need to get readers ready to record their chosen books onto cassette tapes. He was grateful for the opportunity and while working for me, he became a loyal and trusted employee.

In order to be assigned as a tutor in the school, he needed to get a work shift, have it approved by his parole officer and by the work shift board. All of this was accomplished very quickly and he was able to come to work at the school. All of the inmates that I hired to work in the school were assigned as tutors. Turning a New Page Reading Coaches, Cracking the Code Instructors, Turnaround Coordinators and Turning a New Page Sewers, Fabric Cutters and Pressers were titles that I used to describe the jobs that the inmates did for me. Sometimes one person would work in more than one position, filling in wherever I needed him. These titles did not exist in the Offender Management System (OMS) because these positions were not available in other institutions.

Remember my coordinator, Tony, from the Literacy Days chapter? This story is about him. This is how he came to be employed at the school.

Tony was in charge of that Literacy Day project and did a great job for me. He may not have been cut out to work with cows, but the dairy's loss was my gain. Tony spent the rest of his sentence working for me, and I never regretted hiring him. In the course of some of our chats, I found out that he had been good friends with my eldest son, Joe, in high school. Unfortunately, I was not able to share that information with Joe due to privacy issues. Like all of my students, tutors, and Turning a New Page coordinators, I do not know where Tony is or how he is doing today. I always followed the CSC's rule of no contact after release.

Wherever Tony is, I hope he isn't working with cows, and I hope he is successful and happy.

One afternoon, shortly after 1:30 p.m., everyone in class was working quietly while I was working at my desk. Although quiet chatting was permissible in my class as long as work was getting done, there was no chatting going on at all. The class was completely quiet.

Over the next few minutes, there were intermittent squeals.

Finally, I said, "Whoever is making that squealing sound, please stop."

"It's a pig," said one student, Glen.

"Okay, no name-calling. Just stop making that noise," I said.

"I'm not name-calling. Miss, it really is a pig. Bernie has a piglet down the front of his bibbed overalls!" exclaimed Glen.

Now, I was alarmed. "Bernie, is that true?"

"Yes, Miss. He gets lonely in the piggery without me."

"Bernie, take him back there right now. The supervisor must wonder where he is." As Bernie was leaving with the piglet, I said, "I wouldn't think I would have to post the rule 'no pigs in class.'"

Glen said that he wouldn't remark on that since I had said no name-calling. I must say that class at Westmorland Institution was never dull or boring.

When CSC decided to close the farm at Westmorland Institution, the staff, inmates, and surrounding community held protests. Everyone tried to change the minds of the powers that be, but to no avail. The decision had been made because the farm jobs were deemed not viable outside of prison in the "real world." But from an educational standpoint, I observed how much more responsible my students—who worked half-time on the farm—became.

Closing the farm significantly reduced the number of jobs at the institution and led to inmates lying around idle throughout the day. This was not good for anyone. Lying around, unproductive, leads to boredom. In a prison setting, boredom leads to rule-breaking, short tempers, and ultimately more inside crime. When inmates were challenged by work, school, or programs, they were calmer and more content—they felt better about themselves and were able to interact more appropriately. Reducing work sites in a prison is never a good idea.

Turning a New Page offered many varying job positions at Westmorland Institution. Along with providing an artistic vent for myself as supervisor, Turning a New Page allowed me to offer challenging but rewarding work activities. I never encountered a problem among my employees. They all joined together in working for the good of the school children whom we were helping with our book recordings and over-the-chair bags.

That said, I don't think Westmorland Institution has ever recovered from closing the farm. The farm offered unique experiences that no school setting is able to.

CHAPTER 22

Presentations

Presenting in Las Vegas

As part of Turning a New Page, I attended a conference in Las Vegas with Rick and one of his company's employees, Darryl, and Rick's colleague, Lynnette, who had joined us on the Douglas trip. I presented to a group of principals, vice-principals, and school board supervisors. I informed them about the inmates at Westmorland Institution who were reading to fluency through repetition. I mentioned that while improving their own reading skills, the inmates were giving back to the community at the same time.

In corrections, nobody knows or cares about universal test scores to prove that there is quantitative value in what is happening in the classroom. We know inmates are progressing when they complete a level and move on to the next level or receive their GED certificate. We are all concerned about "best practices" (qualitative data). If a practice works well for a teacher in one institution, the teacher should share it so teachers in other institutions may also profit.

As I was presenting, I noticed that the audience was not at all interested in anything I was saying. Their eyes were glazing over, and some were actually nodding off. In midstream, I switched up what I was saying to discuss quantitative data, explaining how we pre- and post-tested our readers and discovered that everyone participating in the "reading for children program," showed some degree of improvement. Post-testing results showed an increase in two to four grade levels for the weakest readers. Now these inmates were reading well enough to complete levels one and two at school. Some inmates, who started at higher levels but were weak readers, improved enough to pass the GED tests and earn a certificate. All of this was due to reading and comprehension improvements.

Now I had every person in the room looking alert and asking questions! For me, it was eye-opening and magical. My presentation was saved.

When we went out to eat that evening, Rick, Lynnette, and Darryl told me that I had done a good job. I knew they were being kind. I told them they would see a huge difference the next day as I had two more presentations to give. I did much better and had everyone on board from my first word to my last. I had learned a value lesson in "knowing your audience." Rick, Lynnette, and Darryl admitted that I did a much better job on the second day. I vowed to always consider my audience in any future presentations.

Presenting in West Virginia

A couple of years later, with Turning a New Page going strong, I applied to present at a conference for the Correctional Educators Association (CEA) of which Canada is a member. That year, the annual conference was being held in West Virginia. Rick also applied to present and host a booth, which would be run by Darryl, the employee who had been with us in Las Vegas. We were both accepted, and I started putting together a video presentation, which I worked on at Westmorland Institution. Rick was also putting together a video highlighting his work as a reading consultant. Over the next couple of months, we were in contact by email and phone, tweaking our presentations.

We both presented during the final afternoon of the conference. I went first, and my presentation was a big hit. I was in my element; I understood what correctional educators wanted to hear. They were so enthused by my presentation that they ran down the stairs to Rick's booth for more information on how to achieve the same results at their institutions. It was so exciting for me. Jean Guy Bourque, CSC's regional manager of correctional programs from the greater Moncton area—my area—was in attendance, and he was pleased to see himself in the video presentation as I included footage of him attending one of our local functions.

After my presentation and a short break, Rick presented in the same room where I had been. Several people who had attended my presentation also attended his. Rick was pointing out how Cracking the Code helped produce better testing results, and he was quoting test scores. I looked around the audience and could see that nobody was paying attention. Nobody was interested in test scores. Just like at my presentation in Las Vegas, some people were nodding off. I caught Rick's eye and realized that he had just noticed the same thing. Again, like me in Las Vegas, he switched up what he was talking about in midstream. He stopped discussing quantitative results and focused on qualitative "best practices," as is known in the correctional system. He quickly woke up his drowsy listeners.

When Rick finished, he received a hearty round of applause and lots of questions. Again, people ran down the stairs to the booth looking for more information based on Rick's presentation. It was really great to see, and we considered it a great success. Rick told me that he now knew what I meant back in Las Vegas when I said I hadn't been talking to my audience.

Rick and I have always had great success in all of our endeavors. He works with children and teachers, while I work with inmates. What we have found is that learning is learning, no matter the age of the individual. When learning takes place, it is always something to celebrate and a source of pride and accomplishment for both the learner and the teacher.

CHAPTER 23

Workshops at Westmorland

During our first few years of running Turning a New Page (2000 to 2005) we received excellent support from both the warden at Westmorland Institution and the early years supervisors from School District 2. The supervisors saw the benefits of the Turning a New Page project for all of us, so they allowed their teachers to attend workshops whenever we offered them. These teachers took part in a very worthwhile way.

One of the teachers told me that she intended to go back to her class and reconsider the needs of a couple of her students. She said that she had gained great insight from an inmate who sat at her table and expressed how hard learning had been for him. The inmate went on to say that after being told he was too dumb to learn, he had accepted this as the truth and stopped trying. "Too dumb to learn" were his words, whether they were actually said to him or he implied them from how he was treated. Why should he try when professionals were telling him he had no chance? But when he got assigned to Westmorland Institution's School, the teachers did not accept that he couldn't learn and set out to prove that not only could he learn, but also, he could excel. He said he had never felt so confident—and for him, this was really a good way to feel.

While sitting at tables composed of inmates and public-school teachers, both groups were able to feel respected, heeded, and valued. In our early days, it was important that our Turning a New Page participants felt that the work they were doing was valuable. Having public-school teachers listen and heed the inmates' words did more for the inmates' self-esteem in a two-day workshop than we could provide in the classroom in a year.

We are still thankful that the school district's supervisors saw the big picture and were so generous in allowing their teachers to participate. A few years later, after Eric Peters had retired, the next supervisor, Carmen Peters, Eric's wife, shared the same vision, but she only held the position for a short while.

When Katherine (Jacks) Arsenault held that position. She was always supportive of our endeavors and our partnership.

By this point, the decision for allowing teachers to attend workshops was being made by the District Board Office. This manager would not allow her teachers to participate in our workshops, and she did not enable our efforts with the district. Fortunately, we never lost the support of Katherine or of the teachers who continued to be part of the Turning a New Page lending program. If these teachers had been allowed to attend our workshops, they would have continued to do so.

These workshops were always offered free of charge to the teachers. The teachers had to travel to Westmorland Institution, but there was no registration price. This meant that for two days they could participate in discussion and hands-on-practice to make their classes more enjoyable and easier to follow.

At one of the workshops, Rick announced that he was going to focus on the Three Rs. He started talking about how the Three Rs were pertinent and how each had an effect on the other.

After several minutes, one of my students asked, "What does this have to do with the Three Rs?"

Rick said that reading affected writing, and both affected arithmetic. Reading, 'riting, and 'rithmetic, the three Rs

"But what does that have to do with the Three Rs?" the student asked again.

Not wanting to take attention away from the discussion at hand, Rick said he would talk about it again after the session if the student still didn't understand it.

Later that day, Rick was making a phone call from my classroom when he noticed my "Three Rs" sign concerning respect in the classroom. Rick finished his call and immediately found me to ask why I hadn't mentioned this sign to him. I honestly had not thought about it during the workshop because I knew about the Three Rs he was referring to. He said it was no wonder the student thought his discussion had nothing to do with the "Three Rs."

In Rick's workshops, he always talks about "viewing," which means that when communicating, both parties need to be aware of what they are talking about. He stresses to teachers the importance of ensuring that students understand the basic concepts before moving on.

This was a perfect example of the two parties "viewing" two entirely different things. One party was viewing the Three Rs as reading, 'riting, and 'rithmetic—and the other viewed the Three Rs as my classroom decorum. This is the funny story I alluded to when explaining the Three Rs back in Chapter 1.

Reader, I am sure that as you read this, you remember a time when you were talking to someone, and at some point, you and the other person realized you were not on the *same page* as you were both talking about entirely different things. At that point, you probably laughed, clarified, and moved on.

Sometimes students are not able to arrive at that stage, and therefore, they must move on without clarification and without having learned.

On one occasion while private tutoring, I was working on the Pythagorean theorem with a Grade 10 girl, Lauren Kinnie, the daughter of one of my best friends, Denise Kinnie. I explained that to use the formula, you must work with right-angled triangles. We talked about the formula, and I was sure that she understood what we were doing.

Then, we moved on to the sample questions she had been assigned at school to prepare for the test the following day. She wrote down the formula, we read the question together, and then I asked her to plug the numbers into the formula so that she could solve the problem. Lauren sat silently looking at the formula and then looking at the problem. She did not attempt to plug the "known values" into the formula. I sat there, waiting.

Finally, I asked if she wanted to review it. She said yes. We reviewed everything from the start. Then, I asked her again to work with the formula. She said she couldn't. I asked her why, and she responded that she didn't know if it was a right-angled triangle or a left-angled triangle. When she said that, I was relieved, because that was the best information she could have given to tell me exactly what it was that she didn't understand. I told her, then, that the orientation did not matter. A right angle is an angle that measures 90 degrees—an angle that could fit into a corner of a page.

With that, she quickly plugged the numbers into the formula and worked out the solution. She completed the 10 practice questions correctly within a few minutes. She made only one minor error on the test the next day, attesting to her complete understanding of the theorem.

Our tutoring session was a moment that demonstrated "viewing" in its most basic form.

When Rick came to the institution to do workshops, he would usually stay for a few days. When not working at the workshops, he would help out in the school with whatever I needed. One afternoon, he and I were both in my classroom with my 12 students. Rick was sitting at my desk correcting some tests. I was sitting halfway back in one of the student desks working on some classroom posters. It was quiet in the classroom with everyone working on their own.

One student, Seth, who sat in the front row right in line with my desk, would repeatedly complain. This was not something new. The other students and I always ignored him. In a whiny voice he would say,

"I'm so sick and tired of being sick and tired…."

On this particular afternoon, after he had said it two or three times, Rick addressed him and said,

"You need to stop saying that. Just work quietly."

Seth didn't respond but a couple of minutes later,

"I'm so sick and tired of being sick and tired…."

"I told you to stop saying that," Rick said.

Again, a couple of minutes later,

"I'm so sick and tired of being sick and tired…"

"WILL YOU PLEASE SHUT UP!" yelled Rick.

Seth literally shook. He just looked at Rick with his mouth wide open and shook from head to toe. You could have heard a pin drop in the classroom.

I was shocked to hear Rick address a student in that manner, but I realized that he had just had enough. I must say that I never heard Seth complain again about being sick and tired.

Another time when Rick was at the institution to do workshops, I was really busy with some paperwork that was time sensitive and had to be in that day. I usually read to my class from 11 a.m. to 11:30 a.m., when school got out for the morning. I told Rick that I could not take the time to do it on this particular day and he volunteered to do it in my place. I was reading a classic Inuit book and had a marker at the chapter where he should begin.

Rick went to my class and informed them that he would be doing the reading that day. He started in and the book was talking about how the Inuit husband had been away for several days on a hunting trip. He returned home, greeted his wife and children and once the children were in bed in the igloo, he and his wife waited for them to be asleep. The story went on quite graphically to describe what he and his wife did next. Rick peeked up over the book and saw 12 sets of eyes interestedly staring at him. He read, "… then they went to sleep and the sun came up the next morning," followed by, "Class dismissed!"

Rick came to my office and said,

"What kind of book are you reading to your class, anyway?"

I thought he was kidding because I had never come to anything like that. It always talked about the hunt and snaring food for his family and how hard it sometimes was, etc. When I looked at what Rick had started to read, I couldn't believe it. Rick thought I had set him up to read that part, but I was not even aware of it. And, nothing else in that book was anything like that. Have I mentioned that we had lots of fun whenever Rick visited us at Westmorland?

CHAPTER 24

Tattoo Stories

One morning while everyone in class was working, I was sitting at my desk and working on math formula posters that I planned to put up on the walls for quick reference. To my left, a tutor was quietly working with a student on English grammar. At the back of the class, three students were working together on math. These students were quietly chatting about various topics when I became aware that they were talking about tattoos. But I was not really listening, and I was not part of the conversation.

Then Jim, one of the three students, addressed me.

"Rosemary, I have to tell you my tattoo story," Jim said.

I looked up and nodded.

"I wanted to get a bumblebee tattooed to my member," he began. "Do you know what I mean?"

"Yes, I know what you mean, but wouldn't that hurt?" I asked in horror.

"I had a plan for that. I went to the tattoo artist with two of my buddies. I picked out the bumblebee that I wanted and informed the artist that I would be back. Then, we went to the liquor store, and I bought a 40-ouncer of Jack Daniels. We went to my apartment, and I drank the whole thing. I was really out of it, but my buddies had not had anything to drink, and they knew what I wanted. As planned ahead of time, they took me back to the tattoo artist. He set up his tools. I was lying on his table. He was all set and with his first stab of the needle, I was off that table like a shot—there's not enough Jack Daniels in the world to lie still for that."

"That was quite an experience. I'm surprised you thought it was a good idea in the first place." I said.

"I wasn't just doing it for myself—I thought the ladies would be all over me to see 'Stinger.'"

"Okay, I think it's time we all got back to work," I said.

I was surprised that Jim would share this story in class because in my mind, it revealed a huge error in judgment. But he did not seem to view it the same way. He told it with a certain degree of bravado that seemed to be shared by the other students.

Tattoos have become very popular in society over the past 20 years. These days, it is not uncommon to see people from all walks of life with tattoos—from tiny tattoos to full sleeves and everything in between. Now it is even called "body art."

It used to be that if you saw a tattoo, then you knew the person had been in the service or in prison. In Canada, tattooing in prison is not allowed. But that doesn't mean that the inmates do not do it. The reason it is not allowed is due to the dangers of sharing needles and ink. Sometimes the inmates will take a chance and crudely tattoo themselves or each other. These tattoos are rarely pretty due to the lack of good tools, good ink, tattooing expertise, and adequate materials. Few prison tattoos would be referred to as body art.

For tattooing, the inmates were limited to ink they hoarded from pens. As a teacher, my suspicions were always raised when a student would ask for a pen every day, knowing he could not have possibly used up the pen I had given him the previous day just by writing poetry in his room.

Jim's tattoo story and the following tattoo stories did not occur in prison but rather on the outside before they were sent to Westmorland Institution.

One afternoon, my student, James, told me that his brother had been approved to come to Westmorland Institution from higher security. James said that his brother would be taking the level two class, and therefore, he would also be my student.

Over the next few days, every time an inmate I didn't know appeared at my classroom door, I would ask James if it was his brother.

"No, Miss. You'll know my brother when you see him."

I asked how this could be so when I had never met him and had not been given a description of him.

"Just remember, I said this: you'll know him when you see him," James said.

I thought they must look so much alike I couldn't miss the similarity. A couple of days later, an inmate I didn't know came to my classroom door.

"James, here is your brother," I said.

James looked up. "Yes, Miss, you're right," he said. "I told you you'd know him when you saw him."

Now here is the rest of the story. James and his brother, Jeremy, could not have looked more different—they had no similarities whatsoever. James had dark hair and almost black eyes; Jeremy was blond with blue eyes. I took a chance guessing it was Jeremy because James kept insisting that I'd know it was his brother.

Jeremy stood out because he had a red heart tattooed in the middle of his forehead. Later, I learned that James and his friends had "branded" Jeremy when he was passed out drunk. James thought he was clever in setting me up to recognize his brother, although he hadn't described him or told me anything about him. He also thought it was great fun sharing the heart tattoo story with the rest of the class.

James and his friend had tattooed Jeremy after he had passed out from drinking, but Jeremy did not even notice the tattoo until he looked in the mirror the next day. This story was less fun for Jeremy, but he was a good sport. He fit right in, and once he got settled, he became a good student.

Several inmates had tattoos of tears on their faces, and I was never sure of the reason why. I did not teach any students with the tears tattoo, but I asked my students if they knew why some chose to have these tattoos.

I got two answers.

Some said that if an inmate lost a loved one while he was incarcerated, he would mark that death with a tear. So, if you saw three tears, it meant that three people important to him had died while he was serving time. The other explanation was that the inmate bearing the tear or tears had killed someone: one tear per death. I am not sure if either of these stories is true, but there was a consensus, among the students in my classroom, that both of these stories were true. One would have to ask the bearer of such tears what his story and reason were.

Outside of inmates, I do not know anyone personally who has facial tattoos. While I am not against tattoos in general, I would not choose to have one myself. I have never understood what could make a person think that getting a facial tattoo is a good idea. There is no way of completely covering your face to hide facial tattoos.

Here is one last tattoo story. Reader, you will ask yourself if this story could possibly be true. As outlandish as this story is, it is definitely the truth.

At Westmorland Institution, we received newcomers at the institution on Thursday mornings. These inmates came from the reception center in Springhill Institution since they needed a minimum-security setting. Or they came after staying in higher security for some time—either months or years—since they were now eligible for minimum-security and were getting ready for release. Staff got notification of newcomers ahead of time.

At the school, the GED teacher, Mike Hodgson, would look up each newcomer in the Offender Management System (OMS) on the computer, and he would advise me of the school level for the offenders on the list. That way, I could ask for students to be assigned to respective classes based on their needs and our availability. They would go before the work shift board shortly after arrival on Thursday and would be assigned to a job, school, or programs starting on the following Monday.

Whenever newcomers arrived at the institution on Thursday mornings, word went around if there was anything out of the ordinary. On one particular Thursday morning, everyone—staff and inmates—were talking about an inmate with an exceptional tattoo. I didn't know anything about him, and since he wasn't on my list of students, he must have already had his high-school diploma. So, although I heard about him, I did not see him.

A couple of weeks later, there was an assembly in the gym for inmates and staff. It just so happened that this inmate was sitting in front of me, to my left. It was a good vantage point for me to see what all the hype was about.

He was not remarkable or noticeable in any way, except for the tattoo he had on his face, neck, and upper right chest. On his right cheek was a snake's head with its mouth open in a hiss, blood dripping down from the fangs. The snake continued down the right side of his face and wrapped around his neck three times with the tail extending to his upper right chest, which was exposed by a low-necked shirt. It was very disconcerting to see this on his face and neck, but it was very well done. I must say that his was the most memorable tattoo I had seen up to that point, and years later it continues to be the most memorable tattoo I've seen to this day.

In hindsight, I would have liked to have known the circumstances of this tattoo. What would possess someone to have a tattoo like that drawn on their face? How did that person feel before, during, and especially after having had it done? Since I never interacted with that inmate, I never did discover the answers to any of those questions. I am not a lover of snakes, but even if I were, never in my wildest imagination would I have something like that drawn on any part of my body, least of all on my face.

There are probably as many different reasons for getting a tattoo as there are people. While some do want body art, I wonder if others just do it for attention. They must want to be noticed, or they certainly would not go to the extent of having big, bright tattoos inscribed on visible body parts. Some things cannot be explained.

CHAPTER 25

Substitute Teachers

In 1996, Bill Snowdon, the education provider for Marshland Educational Services, lost the contract for Westmorland Institution to Excalibur Learning Resource Centre from Markham, Ontario. Robin Quantick, owner of Excalibur, retained Pam Oulton the GED teacher, and me, the level two teacher. Kim Hendrickson, the literacy teacher, chose to continue to work for Marshland Educational Services in Dorchester Medium-Security Penitentiary, where Bill had one teaching position available. Robin hired Scott Jardine to teach the literacy class. In addition to teaching the GED class, Pam Oulton was made the head teacher.

In 2000, Pam left to take another job. This left the head teacher position open. I had been employed by Excalibur Learning Resource Centre for four years as the level two teacher. This position would mean that in addition to being the level two teacher, I would have more outside the classroom responsibilities.

I really wanted this position. I applied and went through the interview process and was really pleased to get the position. This meant that I would need to keep the payroll for myself and the other three teachers: Mary King, who was hired to take Scott's place as the literacy teacher; Scott, who took over as the GED teacher; and Peter Spence, the custodial teacher/ supervisor (explained below). I needed to keep accurate records and submit them each month to Excalibur's head office. I would also need to oversee the general day-to-day happenings in the school. I would report directly to Robin, the education provider and Excalibur's owner.

This was a great honor for me and I was happy to take on the added responsibility.

I was responsible for training and hiring substitute teachers to fill in when one of us full-time teachers wanted a day off or to go on vacation. This was a fun job for me. I would set up a time. Then, the potential substitute would arrive at the prison, and I would show him or her around. I would also go over all the training for teaching in a prison setting and I would explain how to deal with inmates and how not to be taken advantage of in the classroom.

In addition to the three academic classrooms, we also offered a custodial course. This was a 10-week continuous intake program, which offered testing and certification from the province. Since this program was included under the umbrella of the school contract, I was in charge of its administration. We had a staff member, Peter, who oversaw the course's daily teaching and supervision. For the course's classroom study, the student learned basic cleaning skills, as well as how to safely clean blood spills or other bodily fluids. This meant that once released, the certified parolee could be employed by various companies and even hospitals. In addition to classroom participation, the student had to be employed somewhere in the institution as a cleaner. Hence, the participant would acquire book-learned knowledge, as well as practical hands-on work experience.

As I mentioned before, I never knew where released inmates ended up. In one instance, I learned that one of our released inmates had acquired a janitorial position at the Moncton hospital. This job led to him becoming a porter, wheeling patients to x-rays, surgeries, etc. I found out about his success because I was at the hospital for a minor surgery—and he was my porter. It was rewarding to see that he was doing well, had stayed out of trouble, and landed a well-paying job to support his family.

One of the good aspects about being in charge of substitute teachers was that I could hire anyone who was qualified. For the academic classes, I needed to hire someone who was in university working towards a degree. It did not have to be a teaching degree, but it had to be a bachelor's degree. For the custodial course, the substitute teacher only needed to have completed a high-school diploma. Four of my five children worked for me either as a substitute teacher in the classroom or as a supervisor of the custodial course. By the time I got this position, Joe, my oldest son, was already in the job position that he has to this day. So, he never needed to be employed as a substitute for me.

My sons, Jon and Jeff, both substituted as the custodial supervisor. Both worked intermittently a day here and there, and both led a few two-week sessions while Peter was on vacation. While Jon was working on his university degree, he also did some academic substituting. My daughters, Aimée and Alicia, both worked in both the academic classrooms and in the custodial position. They taught at all three academic levels. They both substituted a great deal, and both of them led some long six-week sessions when I or one of the other teachers were out on temporary sick leave. It was great for me, and it really helped them out with funds through the summer months or in between full-time working positions.

My four children were dependable workers and were independent once shown what to do on their first day of work. They did not need to keep checking with me about protocol, and they seemed able to handle the daily activities. It allowed me to witness and appreciate the good work ethic they had developed along the way through school and training.

Jon's girlfriend (now his wife), Liane Fraser, even got to substitute for me one summer. Liane was versatile, did a good job, and was adept at all levels. She worked in the academic classrooms.

As with all of the substitutes, I would spend some time explaining the rules and decorum in the prison setting. As with permanent staff, the substitutes needed to be alerted to dynamic security and not only how to work within the classroom setting, but also how to function in a *prison* classroom setting.

Bill, the education provider at the medium-security prison, Dorchester Penitentiary, said that I did an excellent job of training substitutes.

"Rosemary trains them for substituting, and once they have gotten a bit of experience, I steal them to teach full time in medium," he joked.

It was true.

I could not be upset about it, because a lot of the substitutes I hired were looking for full-time employment. I could not offer that, but he could. His turnaround of teachers was short, with teachers coming and going on a regular basis. At Westmorland Institution, our teaching staff was stable with all of us having worked there for years.

The education provider at Dorchester Penitentiary always said that my substitutes were so well-trained that they could start working for him right away, and he didn't have to do anything extra. But the joke may have been on him because I trained them to work at a minimum-security prison and his was medium security.

One Friday, I had a substitute in working for the literacy class. It was early summer, and the inmates were running a garden center where staff could purchase plants. We—the substitute teacher, Bill MacBeath, and I—went down to the garden center at lunchtime and checked out the plants. We were there for quite a while, and we both bought several plants.

On the way back to the school, Bill told me that he had made a mistake. He told me that an inmate had spent a lot of time working with him and advising him about which plants to use along his walkway. Bill said the inmate was knowledgeable, polite, and helpful. To show his appreciation, Bill tried to offer the inmate a toonie (a two-dollar Canadian coin) as a tip. This freaked out the inmate. The inmate explained to Bill that he could never take money from anyone, and if he did, it could cost him his job—a job he highly valued—and he could possibly get "scooped" (taken to a higher-security prison). The inmate told Bill that it could cause very serious problems for him.

Bill felt terrible that he unknowingly put the inmate in that position. It was good that Bill told me about this incident because I phoned the inmate's work supervisor to report that Bill had made a mistake; I was aware of it, and I had handled it. She appreciated that I phoned her because the inmate had already told her what had happened.

This could have been an incident that would have prevented Bill from returning to the prison. But since he told me up front and right away, we were able to work through it without repercussions. I was glad about this because Bill was, in every way, a dependable substitute teacher, and I would have hated to lose him.

The inmates were aware that I wanted them on their best behavior when I had substitute teachers working in the school. I emphasized that they were to treat the substitute teachers with the utmost politeness and respect.

One summer I was away on a two-week vacation, so I had a young woman substituting in my classroom. When I returned to work, I read the notes she had left me and discovered that my class had really given her a hard time. Every day, there was an incident where she had to pull someone out of class to counsel him or deal with tardiness. To say the least, I was not impressed by this.

When my students arrived in class, I told them how disappointed I was that they had not behaved in a mannerly way. I told them that their usual chatting, which was normally permitted in my class, would not be allowed again until I said so. I told them they would have to work hard to have that privilege restored.

"In the words of Elton John, 'The bitch is back.' Now get to work, quietly," I told them.

Whenever a problem occurs in the classroom and some form of discipline becomes necessary, it would get very quiet. Each student would put his head down, seemingly working on something. The students would not make eye contact with each other or with the teacher. When the teacher says that certain conditions will remain in effect until further notice, there is no argument. When the dust has settled and the teacher is somewhat less irate, one student will tentatively ask when the punishment will be over.

Depending on if the teacher is willing and ready to put the incident in the past or not, I—the teacher—would either give a specific time or say, "When I am satisfied that everyone has gotten the message."

My students really hated it when I was angry with them. They hated it even more when I said they disappointed me. They knew full well the limits that I would accept. But they did not know that with the substitute teachers, and they would always test the limits until the substitute teacher broke.

One morning, I was meeting with a new university graduate who wanted to substitute teach at Westmorland. We sat in my office and I explained what would be expected of her. I went through the training materials with her and she filled out all the necessary paperwork.

Once this was completed, I took her on a tour of the school. I brought her to the literacy class and the GED class and introduced her to the teachers and the students. I showed her my level two class and pointed out where the materials and tests were located.

I showed her the staff room and told her that she could bring her lunch. We had a fully equipped lunch room with a refrigerator and a microwave. I explained that she could also go up to the village of Dorchester, two minutes away, to buy a hot dog or a sandwich at the convenience store. Those were her options.

We returned to my office, and I was set to wrap things up and tell her that she would be hearing from me. At that moment, I looked at her, and she was as white as a sheet. I asked her if she was okay.

This question brought out the tears and shaking.

"I am so scared," she exclaimed in a warbling voice.

"Of what?" I asked.

"Of them," she said.

"Of the inmates?" I was shocked as all the inmates we had encountered that morning were very polite and kind to her, even saying they would look forward to her working in the school.

"I can't help it—I'm terrified of them!" she sobbed.

I told her that I would escort her to the Control Centre to sign out and on the way, we would stop in the printer room to shred all of her paperwork.

"What? You're not going to call me to substitute? I need the money!" she said.

"No job is worth that degree of fear. You should apply to the public-school board. I could not allow you to work here knowing how afraid you are. You would be a risk not only to yourself, but also to the inmates and other staff. Thank you for coming and giving it a try."

I walked her out and this time noted her trepidation just walking through the halls. If I had employed her, she would have had to work in a classroom by herself with 12 inmates. I was thankful to have realized how impossible that would have been for her.

That young woman was the only one to express fear among those that I interviewed. I was fortunate to have an extensive list of very good and very professional substitute teachers.

One substitute teacher that stood out has become a good friend. Myrna Balderston had an exceptional talent for recognizing learning difficulties. She always had an answer for remediating problem areas and finding ways for the students to successfully learn.

Myrna was always available when I called her. She would change her own personal plans to accommodate my need for a substitute at Westmorland Institution. The students respected her and she really enjoyed working with them.

Myrna was just one of the exceptional women and men I was able to employ over the years. My gratitude goes out to each and every one of them.

Over time, I became adept at fitting substitute teachers to the specific classrooms. I had several substitute teachers who could teach any level in any classroom. I had some who preferred teaching the literacy class, which always had fewer discipline problems. My class always seemed to be the most challenging—just like in public middle school or junior high–school classrooms. Young to mid-teens seem to deal with the most drama in their lives, and in my class, since a lot of men encountered many challenges when they were that age attending public school, they did not stay in school. Thus, sometimes my students' emotional development was arrested at that level as they exhibited behavior similar to middle-school children.

In some cases, if they had not come to prison, they would never have gone on to further their education. Being forced to attend school was a very good opportunity for a lot of our inmates.

For the most part, inmates are able to excel far beyond their own expectations when given the chance and proper instruction. Having smaller class sizes than in normal public schools, the teacher has the time and the privilege to explore learning styles to hopefully create a plan for even the most challenging learners. It has been my experience that when school dropouts—"failures" in their own minds—taste a small ounce of success, they are avid to achieve more of that success and more willing to put forth the effort.

In prison teaching, I experienced an "aha" moment every single day. Some were small moments, and others were big moments. All were significant to the learner and proof that he could advance academically. Nothing boosts self-esteem as much as getting something right in school. The more knowledge a student gets, the more he wants.

CHAPTER 26

Random Classroom Happenings

I had a student, Ray, in my class who wore glasses but was having difficulty seeing the board and reading his papers. He was having problems seeing both far and near. I told him to go to Health Care and ask for an appointment with the eye doctor. A week later, he went for an eye exam. He told me that the eye doctor told him that he needed trifocal glasses. I corrected him by telling him he meant bifocal. He said he was sure that the doctor had said *tri* rather than *bi*. Sure enough, when he went to pick up his glasses, they were trifocal. I had never heard of this before.

The eye doctor told him that he may have an adjustment period, but it was normal. I had been talking on the phone to my Mom who had just gotten bifocal glasses, and she was having a terrible time getting used to them. She said she was running into things, and although she was assured that she would get used to them, she did not feel that she was making progress. Knowing this, I encouraged Ray, who was also having a hard time, to stick with it. He was finding it very difficult to see anything at all. He had to take his glasses off to walk from his unit to school and back. He went to Health Care to inquire about it and was told it would just take time for him to get used to the new glasses.

One morning, Ray came to class with a black eye and a cut lip. I did not ask him what had happened because I did not want to report that he had been in a fight. But he volunteered the information that he had been wearing his glasses when he fell down the stairs and smashed his face into the wall at the bottom of the stairs. I really sympathized with him because I, too, had once had vision problems. I did not have any advice for him—other than to hang in there—because the Health Care nurses all told him this was normal.

A few days later, Ray was standing at my desk asking for help with a math problem. He was bent at the waist over the desk, and his head was positioned all the way forward, watching as I wrote the formula. Then, as I was talking to him, he stood up with his head bent at the neck and pointing towards the ceiling. When I realized what he was doing, a horrible thought crossed my mind. I asked him if he had ever talked to the nurse at Health Care while wearing the glasses. He said he had not. He had always taken them off to talk to her. I told him to go and talk to her again with his glasses on. I told him to tell the nurse that his teacher thought that the lenses were inserted upside down.

When Ray went to Health Care and told the nurse what I suspected, she thought the idea was preposterous. But she kept the glasses to show to the eye doctor.

A couple of days later, Ray was paged to Health Care to see the eye doctor who had re-evaluated his glasses. The eye doctor was apologetic and said it was no wonder Ray had had such a difficult time. He reversed the upside-down lenses and thought that Ray would not have any further trouble.

Ray came back to class beaming. He had the biggest smile I had ever seen him have. He walked from Health Care to school with his glasses on and didn't have any trouble at all. He could see well. He told me that he had almost given up as he was tired of running into things and falling down. He had just about decided that he would no longer wear glasses and would just resign himself to not being able to see well. I told him that, in hindsight, it was a little funny that the lenses were inserted upside down. Ray said he did not find it funny right then, but maybe in time he would. He said his bruises were too fresh for humor at that point. The good thing for him, though, was that he appreciated being able to see so well. I don't think I ever saw him again without his glasses on.

One morning just before 8 a.m., my student, Adam, came to the classroom door and asked if he could see me in my office. I asked if it had to be right then because class was about to start. He looked over one shoulder and then the other—he said he really needed to see me right then. I went to my office, and a few minutes later, he joined me. He was nervous. He looked around and asked if he could close the door. I told him he could and I asked what was with all the cloak and dagger. Adam said he needed to show me something, and he placed a $5 bill on my desk. He told me he had found it in the toilet in his unit. I said that he was lucky, and it was a case of "finders, keepers."

But then he told me that it wasn't real. I was looking right at the bill and asked him what he meant by that. He said he meant that it was counterfeit. Not real. Looking at it lying on my desk, I couldn't see anything wrong with it. I picked it up, and as soon as I touched it, I knew that he was right—it wasn't real. So, he asked me what he should do. I told him to leave it with me. I would write up an incident report and turn both the bill and the report in to security. He was relieved and thanked me. Then he left and went back to class.

Before turning the bill and the report in to security, I showed it to some co-workers in the staff room. The bill was unbelievably well done. We had a fairly good photocopier in the school, but it could not have done such a good job with a double-sided bill. It was right on. Not even a bit out of line. I didn't think it could have been assembled within the institution, but some staff said that other departments had some very high-end printers.

While showing the bill, the GED teacher, Scott, came into the room and asked what was going on. I told him the story, and he was very interested. He was examining the bill with great curiosity when he asked me again where it was found. When I told him that it had been found in the toilet in one of the inmate units, he dropped it on the floor and immediately went to the sink to wash his hands. This made me laugh.

Once I turned the bill over to security, I did not find out anything else about it. I inquired, but I was told that it was taken care of. I did not find out if it had been made on site, who had made it, or anything else about it. I guess it was above my pay grade.

One Monday, my new student, Mark, came to class, and whenever he spoke, he used a great deal of profanity. I explained to him that he needed to use business English while in class. He asked why, and I told him that he needed to use appropriate language as practice for getting a job once released. And I preferred not to hear profanity in my classroom. He said he would try but that he always spoke like that and did not hold out hope that he could do better. I told him that I was happy that he agreed to try.

Over the next few days, Mark's language was totally inappropriate in class. I called him on it, and he said he had warned me that he probably wouldn't be successful in using appropriate language—he said that was just how he was, and I would need to accept it. Really? This was my classroom!

I told Mark I would give him until the end of the week to improve and clean up his language. He asked what would happen then. I told him that if his language had not improved by Friday, then the following Monday I would give him a list of 10 vocabulary words each day. He would need to write two sentences with each word and learn to spell all 10 by the end of the day.

"That will be my punishment?" Mark asked.

"No, it's not a punishment. You obviously have a very limited vocabulary consisting mostly of profanity. This will improve your vocabulary, and at the end of each week, you will have learned 50 new words. Then, you will have more words at your disposal, and hopefully you will be able to express yourself without swearing."

He asked what he needed to do in order to avoid learning 10 new words a day. I told him he would need to speak in class without cursing and swearing.

"But as you have told me, I know you can't do that, so I will have your word list prepared for Monday," I told Mark.

"I'll f—king do it. You'll see," he said.

"You're off to a good start, Mark. Sorry, but my money's on Miss for this one," another student chimed in.

That was the last profanity I heard from Mark. He did not want the extra work, and to my great surprise, I never heard a foul word from him again in class. It just goes to prove how much an effort someone will make when it matters to them!

One of the Grade 7 math modules dealt with measurement. In addition to rulers, I had a meter stick in my classroom to use for measuring in this module. This stick stood in the corner tucked in beside the file cabinet.

Harry, one of my students, was very hyper and found it hard to sit still for any length of time. I advised him to take short walks in the hall when sitting got to be too much. If the meter stick was in its proper place by the file cabinet, Harry would not touch it. If it was across a desk or, in view, leaning against the wall, Harry would pick it up and poke other students with it or use it as a pool cue to knock things off his desk.

One morning, the administrative assistant came to my door and motioned that she would like to talk to me. I went out into the hall to meet with her.

"You know that blind student in your class?" she asked.

"No, I don't have a blind student in my class," I said.

"Yes, I asked him and he said he was in your class," she told me.

"I don't have a blind student, but what happened?"

"Well, I was walking in the hall on my way to the staff room. He was coming towards me, tapping his stick. He couldn't see me, so I went up against the wall and called out to him, saying, 'Watch out. I'm here. Don't run into me.' I was afraid he would bump into me and fall down."

"Wait a minute—the stick he had—was it a meter stick?" I asked.

"I'm not sure. I wasn't paying attention to that. I just felt bad that he couldn't see. When I spoke to him, he was looking all around, but he told he was in your class," she explained.

I thanked her for letting me know. I had figured out that the "blind guy" was Harry with the meter stick. I spoke to him and told him that he had scared her. He was very apologetic and wanted to run to her office to tell her he was sorry. I told him that I would tell her and he should avoid such shenanigans in the future.

On yet another Monday morning, one of my newcomers, Ken, arrived from the medium-security reception center in Springhill Institution. He had been in the Springhill facility school, and his teacher had been Janice. When he arrived in my class, he told me that he didn't think he could be successful without his teacher, Janice. I told him that I would be his teacher now, but he could also receive help from the other two teachers in the school or from one of the several tutors in the school.

Ken was upset that he would have to work in the classroom without Janice. I took it easy on him because I knew how attached some students became to their teachers. I understood that this was not put on and not something they planned. I had noted that when some students came to my class from the literacy class, they would pop in to the literacy class several times a day to touch base with their literacy teacher, Mary. To a lesser extent, when my students advanced to the GED class, they would do the same by coming by to say hi to me on their way in or out of the school.

When my students were close to completing my class, I would hype up the completion as a major achievement and tell them how great it was that they had accomplished all of the objectives set out in level two. I would tell them how proud they should be to advance to the GED class and how well-prepared they were for their next step.

So, when Ken arrived in my class, I was determined to help ease the transition from his former teacher to me. I was patient with him and tried encouraging him as much as I could. At the same time, I did not want to enable him to stay stuck. He needed to move on. Every day, he would lament the fact that Janice taught him this way or that way, and he could not quite understand my methods.

Two weeks into this, my patience was wearing thin. I still tried to encourage him as much as I could, but I did need him to start doing some work, start writing some tests, and start making some progress. He came to me and said he just didn't know what to do.

"Look, Ken, we're going into the second week where you have done nothing but complain. Do the work or don't do it. I don't care. But do it or don't do it quietly. No more complaining."

He looked at me, crestfallen. "What? You don't care. Rosemary, you really don't care? How can I make you care?" he asked.

"Get to work, do a test, and give me results to write in your monthly report," I said.

What Ken never knew was that his response almost made me cry. He was so in need of someone—anyone—caring. He got to work and did very well.

Every day, he would ask me if he was doing enough for me to care again. Other students would get a bit fed up with his neediness.

One day, when Ken asked the question again, another student, Roger, turned to him.

"Yes, Ken, she cares. You pushed her too far and that's why she said she didn't care. She did care then, and she cares now. If she didn't care, she wouldn't be here. Now stop asking if she cares. Just know that she does," Roger said.

"Thank you, Roger, for the endorsement. Now, we have three days before the end-of-the-month reports. Please check last month's report and see if you all have met your monthly goals. Back to work."

As I mentioned, some students got very attached to their teacher and at the same time, they also became very protective. One day during lunchtime, I needed to go to the main building for a quick meeting. It was a Tuesday, so the inmates were lined up to receive their pay. As I was walking through, one of the inmates made a catcall and whistled. I just kept walking, but all of a sudden, I heard,

"Hey, man, that's my teacher … Show a little respect."

"Oh, sorry, man, I didn't know; it won't happen again," said the whistler.

I kept walking, and since my back was to them, they couldn't see the big smile on my face. I found it so funny that the whistler would apologize, not to me, but to my student.

CHAPTER 27

Statistics

Being the head teacher, I was in charge of filling in the monthly statistics in the computer's Offender Management System (OMS) each month. Each teacher had a sheet to fill with the names of newcomers for the month, the number of test completions, the number of level completions, and the number of parolees.

The other two teachers and the custodial supervisor submitted their monthly reports to me on the last working day of the month. I kept a running tally on a universal template, which my superiors and administrators could access on the computer. In Ottawa, if educational supervisors wanted to know what was happening in the school at Westmorland Institution, they could simply click on OMS, choose Westmorland in the institutional dropdown menu, and then choose the school. From there, they could see at a glance how many students we had and any other pertinent information about the group in general or a certain student in particular. It was my responsibility to make sure this information was up-to-date at all times.

Although I have talked about "best practices" and being concerned more about qualitative than quantitative data, we still had to show that we were producing good results in order to justify our very existence. Every organization has bean counters: people who consider numbers to be all important. And I recognize that they do have their place.

In saying that we—the teachers—did not worry about quantitative data, I do not mean that we totally disregarded it. Rather, we just believed that if our qualitative data was strong, the quantitative data would be too, since it was in direct proportion and as a result of said qualitative data.

We strove to offer rewarding experiences within the classroom and with programs like Turning a New Page. If we could get the students to buy into putting forth an effort to learn, everything else would fall into place.

At the end of the year, I was responsible for inputting our yearly statistics into OMS. The interesting thing to me was that from year to year the data did not change much. Names changed, but the numbers were quite consistent.

I will focus here on the statistics from my own class because statistics from the other two classes and the custodial course were similar.

Every year, my class had between 50 and 55 students. I had 12 students on a continuous intake basis. I always had between 35 and 38 completions. This is an average success rate of between 61 percent and 69 percent.

This success rate may seem low, but it all depended on the length of stay in the classroom. Sometimes I only had a student for a couple of weeks or a couple of months. There were many reasons for this: parole, disciplinary higher security, work release, and programs, to name a few.

Averaging 55 students a year means that in my 25 years of working as a correctional educator—teacher—I worked with approximately 1,375 inmate students. It is my hope that their success rate in the community has exceeded my yearly completion rate. Hopefully, going to school at Westmorland Institution was the highlight of their incarcerated experience.

CHAPTER 28

Teamwork to Achieve Reintegration

When Mike Corbett was made warden of Westmorland Institution in 2000, he came with an agenda to make some positive changes. At the time, two outstanding factors about the Atlantic Corrections were in need of amelioration.

1. Regional District Commissioner (RDC) Alphonse Cormier wanted Westmorland's operational performance improved with respect to successful reintegration. At that time, Westmorland's day parole numbers were on par with CSC's other minimum-security facilities nationally, but the institution's parole suspension and revocation rates were unacceptable and the work release numbers were the worst in the country.

2. Alphonse and Mike shared the belief that institutions are at a distinct disadvantage when it comes to preparing inmates to succeed in the community. They both believed that "crime is a community problem," and "reintegration is a community solution."

Alphonse and Mike made a commitment to have as many inmates in, and contributing to the community in order to learn to embrace community values and work attitudes. It was also a dynamic way to introduce restorative justice initiatives to our offenders. This is the reason why Westmorland Institution took on projects like restoring of Dorchester's historic graveyard; helping to renovate the village's community center;

producing "burial urns for pets" in Westmorland's ceramics shop and donating them to the Moncton SPCA as a fund-raising initiative for that organization; helping to build Irishtown Park; and a number of other initiatives. With all of this going on at Westmorland, we came on the scene with our idea for Westmorland's Literacy Project, another inroad to the community. As mentioned before, Warden Corbett embraced this project and supported us well past the project stage into the program of Turning a New Page.

We were able to further join the team in working towards rehabilitation. It was a great honor to be part of the initiative going forward and as highlighted in previous chapters, we contributed to the best of our abilities.

Through all of these initiatives, the hard work of all staff and the great participation from all of the inmates involved, by 2004, Westmorland Institution had achieved:

- the most work releases and community involvements of any CSC institution in Canada
- the highest day parole grant rate of any CSC facility in Canada
- the lowest parole suspension and revocation rates in the country
- the highest rate of random drug tests per population in the service
- the lowest number of positive drug test results from these tests

This has just been an overview of how much good was coming from Westmorland Institution at that time. Not having worked there for the past number of years, I cannot attest to its continued efficiency, but my hope is that there are still innovative activities in which inmates may participate. I know that there are many challenges due to COVID-19. Fortunately, to date, there have not been any cases for either staff or inmates in our Atlantic prisons. I do not know how this virus has affected the institution's ability to offer community outreach events. But I am sure that staff are working diligently to continue the good progress and to meet the objectives of the CCRA and its mission statement.

CHAPTER 29

The End of Turning a New Page

When Mike retired as warden of Westmorland Institution, I started having difficulty continuing Turning a New Page. Mike saw the vision and benefits of the program right from the start. He ensured that I had what I needed to promote the program. He acted as a liaison between the institution and the public-school district. I could always count on him.

The Interim Acting Warden, Sandy Ward, also offered greatly appreciated support. When the next warden, whom I shall not name, came on board, she did not see the big picture. She did not seem to care that we had made serious inroads with the public or that Turning a New Page continuously presented good news. Where the media likes to focus on how "horrible" inmates are, Turning a New Page always garnered good press and always presented the good work that our inmates were capable of doing. The new warden did not recognize this and put up blockers at every turn. She originally did it quite subtly, but as time went on, she made it harder and harder for us to continue the program.

The first—not-so-subtle—big blocker she put up was that she suddenly forbade me to hire sex offenders for any part of the program, even the sewing part. We employed quite a few sex offenders, and all of them were excellent workers. Way back at the beginning of the program, we had met with Eric Peters and Terry King, the early years supervisors. At that time, we had discussed that no crime, let alone a sex offense, would ever be an issue for the children. No child would ever come in direct contact with one of our inmates. We never strayed from that guarantee, and we never had any issue with the public concerning this matter.

For whatever reason, the new warden did not accept this and would not allow us to hire sex offenders for any Turning a New Page jobs. We could not even hire them to work on the turnarounds or any element of the sewing project.

This was a giant blow to the program because there are a lot of sex offenders at Westmorland Institution. Not being able to hire any of them cut back on our resources tremendously. The warden did not even have the good grace to inform me of this new rule. I had to learn about it through the work shift board when I asked for employees for the program. I cannot say for certain, but it felt like it was her intention to shut us down.

Another issue for the program was that we—the teachers—were not federally employed. As mentioned before, we were contracted and worked for the Ontario-based Excalibur Learning Resource Centre, owned and operated by Robin Quantick. It was a great company to work for, and Robin was very good to all of us. The only problem was that every five years, companies had to bid on providing the educational services. Even if the company's teachers were doing a great job, the contract could only be retained if the company put forth a proposal and was then chosen to continue on for another five years.

As contracted teachers, we were never sure if Excalibur would be able to secure the contract, so we were always very agitated and unsure if we would still have jobs at the end of the five years. This would cause major stress.

All of the materials that belonged to Turning a New Page belonged to Rick, and the materials were available to me as long as I worked there. If I were to leave, I would have to secure those materials and get them out of the prison.

In 2010, I decided to shut down Turning a New Page at Westmorland Institution. We were very unsure if we would get the contract. Robin was doing his best, but could not give us any guarantees. It would have been way too much material to move in a day or two if we did not get the contract. Since I was driving a Toyota Corolla at the time, I had a back seat and a trunk. I got my employees to pack and load materials each day for two weeks. It was heartbreaking to have to shut down our book-lending services, as well as our sewing services. It was difficult to let my workers go—they had been such dedicated employees.

As it turned out, we got the contract for another five years, but since it was only one factor standing in our way, I decided not to bring Turning a New Page back, thinking it would only raise false hopes. It was a tremendous program that lasted more than 10 years, and it was really fulfilling work for both me and all the inmates I employed during our successful run. I am grateful for the support of staff who *got it* as that was the majority. I am also thankful for the inmates who took on anything I asked and did a great job without complaint. They helped me tremendously, but more importantly to them, they helped lots of children.

CHAPTER 30

Retirement

I retired on September 30, 2015, after 25 years of working in a job that I loved. Starting out, I could have never known how important and rewarding this job would be for me. My title *Just Call Me "Teacher": A Memoir about My Career as a Correctional Educator* refers to the fact that in Canadian correctional settings, teachers are referred to as correctional educators. That is fine, but when someone asks, "What do you do?" and you say, "I'm a correctional educator," sometimes they still do not know what you do. Nobody wonders what you do if you say, "I'm a teacher." To be honest, I really like the word *teacher* and I was honored to be known as one.

Since retiring, I have spent more time with my family. My son, Joe, and his wife, Heather (Prosser), and their two sons, Dylan and Jake; my daughter, Aimée, and her husband, Stephen Lockie, and their two children, Emma and Ethan; and my son, Jon, and his wife, Liane (Fraser), and their two children, Ava and Lukas, all live close by, here in Riverview. My daughter, Alicia, and her husband, Dave Kane, live about an hour and a half away in Whitney, part of the Miramichi; and my son, Jeff, and his wife, Josée (Bourque), and their little girl, Maggie, live about 25 minutes away in Memramcook. I am fortunate in that all of my children have chosen to live close by. We presently total 19. The seven grandchildren are accessible, and we are able to attend their birthday parties, sports, and musical, dance, and martial arts events. We are able to have family get-togethers for all of the major holidays and make an effort see each other often in between.

I have enjoyed activities, such as swimming and sewing, and I have spent the last four years trying to learn to ice skate. It is very difficult, and I am not very good, but so far, I have remained upright.

My husband, Barry, and I had traveled a bit before I retired. But since my retirement, we have traveled quite a bit more. We try to do two trips a year—both in the off-seasons of spring and fall. That way we are able to avoid crowds and lineups and spend the best parts of our year, weather-wise, right here. This year, due to COVID-19, we have remained at home.

I have also spent the last few years writing this memoir. It has been fun for me to remember some of the funny incidents you have just read about. Going forward, I hope this inspires some young graduates to consider becoming correctional educators. CSC needs more young people to commit. I guarantee that it will be a rewarding career!

CONCLUSION

As noted, I had some great experiences in my career as a teacher (correctional educator). I worked with some very talented men and have had the honor of teaching them some academics, which they had missed out on along the way. Early on in working at Westmorland Institution, I was constantly amazed by the vast amount of knowledge, insight, and talent exhibited in the prison population. Having worked there for 25 years, I stopped being surprised by the rate of professionalism and effort the inmates were willing to exhibit. Right up to my last day working there, though, I never ceased to be pleasantly awed by it.

I would like to think that I made a difference for the better in my students' lives. I know that working with them made me recognize the value of people, no matter what their deficits may be. I believe that I learned as much from them as they did from me.

I hope you have enjoyed my musings and that it gave you a bit of insight into the school system within a prison. As I have related, a lot of good things can and do happen within such schools.

Thank you, readers.

RP

June 2020

I must add an aside to my conclusion. This is an experience that happened just a few days ago. My husband, Barry, and I were walking on a trail in the woods in our community. We encountered a family: a man, his wife, their four-year-old daughter, and their 13-month-old son. The little girl was very personable and wanted to tell us about things they had encountered along the trail.

All of a sudden, her dad said to me, "You're the teacher."

"I didn't teach in public school," I said.

"No, you taught inside. You were my teacher." He turned to his wife and said, "This is the teacher I told you about. She's the one who wouldn't take any nonsense from anyone."

I asked him his name, and he told me it was Sam. I remembered him when he said he had taken my class and gone on to the GED class where he had achieved his GED certificate. He had earned the highest mark on the writing skills portion of any student we had had. I asked him if having his GED certificate had made a difference for him, and he said it made his life a lot easier. His wife was nodding her head *yes* to that. This was good to hear. I could see that he was happy and doing well.

As mentioned before, I was unable to keep in touch with my students after they were released. Random encounters in the community, like this one, are the only ways I'm able to know that my students are doing well. It is ironic that we met Sam just as I was writing the conclusion to my book.

ACKNOWLEDGEMENTS

I would like to sincerely thank former Warden Mike Corbett and former substitute teacher, Myrna Balderston, for proofreading my manuscript and offering great suggestions, which I heeded. I greatly appreciate your efforts.

I would also like to thank Aimée Lockie for taking my picture for the back cover. This was also greatly appreciated.

Finally, last but not least, I would like to thank my entire family for your love and support. You all mean the world to me.

Lightning Source UK Ltd.
Milton Keynes UK
UKHW041829160421
382135UK00008B/580/J